MINDFUL MONDAYS

Transforming the Everyday to Claim Calm and Reduce Stress

KIMBERLY V. DWYER, PH.D.
DWYER PSYCHOLOGICAL SERVICES, PC

Kimberly V. Dwyer, Ph.D.
Dwyer Psychological Services, PC

Printed in the United States of America
First Printing 2021
First Edition 2021

ISBN: 978-1-7373253-0-7

Nothing in the book is the substitute for mental health, legal, or financial advice
as it applies to the reader's specific situation. It is recommended that the reader
consult with professionals within his or her own state for any mental health
advice or legal or financial advice, and the reader takes full responsibility for use
of any content contained in this book in their personal and professional lives.

For J.D.--my one thing.

Table of Contents

Introduction

Let the waters settle and you will see the moon and the stars mirrored in your own being. --Rumi

It is a busy world, between work, home, and society at large. Most of us would do well to invite in more calm. Mindfulness meditation offers us just that; a reset to our central nervous system, the opportunity to evaluate where and how we focus our attention, and the opportunity to shift our awareness.

Before I started meditation practices, I thought meditation offered some elusive, out-of-body experience, a melding with higher consciousness signaled by a sensation of floating off of the floor while surrounded in blue light. Maybe you've had that impression, too. While meditation can be extremely peaceful, spiritual, and other-worldly, it can also be a moment of recognizing that our thoughts are moving quickly, distracting us with mental chatter. That revelation left me wanting. Where's that spiritual communion filling the body with ethereal blue light that I was expecting?

The reality is, mindfulness meditation is the practice of directing one's attention, without judgment, to the present moment. It's that simple... and that complicated. In moments of mindfulness, sometimes the space between thoughts will grow. Sometimes our bodies relax. Sometimes we do feel deeply connected to the world around us. Sometimes, when we use our ability to observe thoughts and feelings, it allows for wisdom to arise. Sometimes our strong emotions offer us a lens into our value system, which we can then use to direct ourselves into aligned action. These moments of insight into our experience provide us the opportunity to claim calm. Perhaps we are even afforded a chance to reduce stress and embrace peacefulness as we learn that accepting our experiences, good, bad, or otherwise, allows us a path forward, while resisting these experiences keeps us stuck.

I love the metaphor of being immersed in water as mindful awareness. Slipping into the stream of present moment awareness and hanging out there for a bit, is akin to a long swim in the ocean, letting the waves pass over you, bobbing along, occasionally getting tossed in the surf. A week-long meditation retreat might feel like a week in the ocean. Sometimes we are only able to attend a weekend retreat that feels like floating along on a lake. Other times our practice is shorter: an hour, thirty minutes. Then bobbing along a river or a stream comes to mind, or maybe a jump into a favorite swimming hole. While all of these practices are meaningful and strengthen mindfulness skills, I'm personally fascinated by our extremely short journeys into mindfulness: the raindrops. I believe the raindrops are where the true power of mindfulness practice lies.

Tiny but plentiful, raindrops represent all the moments of mindful awareness that occur in the midst of our days. Perhaps an awareness of the intensity of the blue sky. A deep inhale of coffee that brings you immediately into the present moment. The soft silky feel of your dog's ears as you pet them. A single breath that resets the body and allows us to access different choices. Those brief moments, like raindrops, are freely available and brief, but abundant when we bring them into focus.

When you add up those raindrops that we can collect over the span of a day, a week, a year, or a lifetime, we find ourselves swimming in a vast and boundless ocean of present moment experience.

In *Mindful Mondays: Transforming the Everyday to Claim Calm and Reduce Stress*, I share what I think of as "raindrop moments": brief strategies to reconnect to present moment experiences during our everyday life. Some strategies will be faster than others, but I've included suggestions on how to pull from lengthier formal meditation strategies into "on the fly" moments of mindful awareness during your busy week. For people in a traditional Monday through Friday rhythm of work, school, and life, Monday offers a perfect opportunity to hit reset, to learn a new skill, and practice it for a limited time period of the week. Of course, you are welcome to start a strategy on any day of the week, and gather raindrops as you see fit to fill your own tub, pool, lake, and, eventually, ocean of present moment experience.

Jump in, the water's fine!

How to use this book

This book is arranged by sections based on focus of awareness and skills. Mindfulness meditation training typically starts with using our senses, our bodies, and our breath as focuses of awareness. We'll start there. You, of course, are free to start wherever you like. But even if you are a skilled mindfulness practitioner, I'd recommend you come back and visit the seemingly-simpler practices. Applying them in different ways and in shorter raindrop-sized chunks may open up new awareness for you.

After mindfulness of breath, body, and senses, we'll move into mindfulness of emotions and thoughts. Bringing our attention to thought and feeling is a very different experience for those who have not tried it. I liken it to taking a step back from the experience and observing how thought and emotion play out in our brains and bodies, as if we are observing the experience for the very first time. Next, we'll examine practices that open up our awareness to our values. Finally, we'll look at day to day applications for these skills and strategies.

Each strategy is presented as a short chapter, in a What--Why--How format. The What: a brief explanation of the practice. The Why: the background or purpose for this practice. Whenever possible, I'll explain the psychology and/or physiology behind the practices being suggested. Finally, The How: how you can implement this practice in short and practical ways.

After each chapter, you'll find a planning and reflection tool. You can use this to strategize how to implement these practices in ways that are meaningful and accessible to your life. You might commit to using a specific strategy in a specific way, and you'll be prompted to problem-solve any barriers to implementation. After spending some time practicing this new skill (I suggest a week) you can reflect on how the strategy worked for you and can be utilized moving forward in your life. Mine your experience and new knowledge for "raindrop opportunities": moments to practice mindfulness "on the fly" as you go about your life, reconnecting to your internal and external world and resetting your central nervous system.

Looking for more content than what you'll find within these pages? Head over to my website, www.drkimdwyer.com/books. Click on the link for *Mindful Mondays*, and you'll find recorded meditations to get you started as well as additional tips and strategies to help you make the most of your journey into mindfulness. You'll also find a printable version of the Reflection and Implementation Tool, especially useful if you are reading on an e-reader.

Reflection and Implementation Tool

My main takeaways from this chapter:

My goal to use this in my own life:

Specific opportunities I may have to use this strategy or skill:

Obstacles to using this skill and meeting this goal:

Reflection and Implementation Tool

How to problem solve these obstacles

My commitment to use this skill (rate 0-10):

After implementation, here is my reflection on how this worked for me:

Raindrop moments where I can use this skill in the future:

Section 1: General Mindfulness Strategies

Chapter 1: Defining Mindfulness

In this section, we'll explore general strategies to strengthen mindful awareness. Mindfulness practices help us direct our attention to the present moment without judgment. There are three important concepts in this definition:

1. Practicing mindfulness is about learning to direct our attention. While other forms of meditation may focus on achieving spiritual connection, mindfulness practices focus on noticing the focus of our attention and working to intentionally direct our attention.

2. Practicing mindfulness is about present moment awareness. In formal mindfulness meditation and in "real life" mindfulness practice, we seek to bring our attention to the present moment.

3. Mindfulness practice seeks to remove judgment. While practicing mindfulness, we seek to attend without engaging in evaluation--good, bad, beautiful, ugly, horrible, perfect, etc. Judgment is the mind's commentary on a situation and not the pure sensations of the moment brought to the mind via the senses. This commentary is often preconceived; based on prior experiences, and not necessarily a reflection of our present moment.

These concepts may be very comfortable to you if you've already practiced mindfulness. If not, you may find it helpful to explore why directed attention to the present moment without judgment is a helpful concept, and why our brain and bodies evolved to focus outside of the present moment, and, at times, with judgment.

It is the habit of the mind, and frankly, the job of the mind, to wander. This is a primitive safety strategy deeply coded into our DNA. From a physiological standpoint, survival of the species is our goal. We need to keep ourselves safe from life threatening danger. The mind that is good at managing safety is the mind that constantly scans the environment. That scanning mind then presents our conscious awareness with tidbits of information to think about. If you're on the savannah with lions and tigers or other predators, constant attention to potential threats is important. Pay attention to these intrusive "lion on the left" tidbits, and you stay safe and alive. Don't pay attention and you may be ambushed and become a lion's lunch. Early humans who didn't pay attention were less likely to live to the age of reproduction. Thus, the DNA of the early humans who had minds that were more prone to scanning and interrupting the conscious mind with safety information was more likely to be passed on to future generations, as the individual's carrying that DNA reached maturity and produced children.

Fast forward six-hundred thousand years, and many humans have moved off of the savannah and into the suburbs and board rooms. We still have threats in our environment, but they are rarely predators. They are more likely to be of the "Hey, if you don't finish those reports by 5pm, your job is on the line" variety. We don't need to be constantly scanning our environment and interrupting our thought processes with "danger!" thoughts. Instead, we would benefit from focused attention without interruption to the task at hand, completing those reports by 5pm. But given that evolution favored the brain that was in constant scanning mode for roughly all but the last 200 years, focused attention is a work in progress for us twenty-first century humans. Mindfulness practices provide us with an opportunity to work on enhancing this skill.

The second part of the mindfulness definition is "to the present moment." Mindfulness practices use the present moment as a source of awareness. This could be the present moment outside of us: information brought into our brain through our five senses. Or it can be the present moment within us: an awareness of our thought processes, of physical sensations within the body, and of our emotions. Why is present moment awareness so important?

Bringing our attention to the present moment allows us to assess how we are doing right now. What's going on in our body? Are we breathing? Is our heart beating? If those two conditions are met, from a biological standpoint we are doing just fine. The highly developed safety centers of our brain, the limbic system and amygdala, to be precise, are very sensitive to both external and internal information about safety.

Try this: allow your mind to focus on an anticipated event or imagined outcome that is somewhat stressful for you. You'll probably notice that your heart rate and respiration (breathing) rate rise. Focusing your mind on this future stressful event sets the "fight or flight" response in motion. However, those events that you are thinking about are future and imagined events, and no amount of cortisol release in the body *right now* will help you fight some future anticipated stressor. And if the stressor is of the "report due by 5pm" variety, the fight or flight response will not be helpful while you're in the process of completing your report; it may actually impair your ability to stay focused on the task.

Refocusing on the present moment often informs the brain that we are ok. Our heart is beating, and we are breathing. Returning to the present moment allows us the internal calm from which we can make measured decisions and take action to align with our goals. Present moment awareness does not mean we never engage in future oriented planning. It does mean that when we engage in future planning, it is just that: planning. Not worrying. Not half of our brain thinking about the future while the other half tries to be present and watch a movie with our family. Dedicated, focused planning about the future is great. The busy brain that tries to problem solve our futures while we try to enjoy a movie and our loved ones' company, or work on our due-at-5pm reports, is not a helpful brain. Mindfulness practices help us bring attention back to the present moment, so that we are fully engaged with the task at hand.

The last portion of the mindfulness definition is "without judgment." This refers to the ability to be an observer of information. Information could be external, things happening around us we recognize through our senses; or internal, our body's sensations and experiences, our thoughts, and our emotions. When we observe without judgement, we do not overlay preconceived notions, expectations, or prior experience on information. Things that are happening are happening right now, as if for the first time, so that we can fully experience them without the additional layers of filtering and judgment that our brain brings in via past experiences.

As an example, take a situation where you wake up in the middle of the night because you hear a car door slam. At its most basic, this is noise;

air waves disturbed and vibrating and brought to your ear where your brain interprets the sound. And being that it is not a "regular" sound for you at night, your brain wakes you up. Assessing the situation in the present moment without judgment, the brain may say, "Oh, car door sound, no problem, go back to sleep." But the judgments laid on by the brain can take you in other directions. For instance, if you layer on, "Oh, those are my neighbors, probably out partying all hours of the night, so inconsiderate. Don't they know that people have jobs to get up for in the morning? Don't they actually work?" You can see how this judgment may not be helpful, may not be based in reality, and likely won't help you return to sleep.

Our brains are very good at fitting new information into old boxes. It's a time saver. If we can overlay an already developed concept onto novel information, we can establish our responses, our thoughts and feelings, to that information more efficiently. This ability is likely one reason that we have thrived as a species; we can think fast and make decisions based on past experience. This is a super important skill while roaming the savannah with possible predators. We quickly identify a rustle in the tall grass as perhaps belonging to a creature that wants to eat us for lunch. But in our modern world, this ability can quickly get us into trouble as we bring to mind past experience that may not appropriately inform our current experience.

For instance, if you had a situation where a friend whom you trusted later betrayed your confidence, you might go into new friendships somewhat guarded. Your mind is taking the "friendship" concept and overlaying the prior experience of betrayal. As the new friendship develops, the old betrayal narrative is activated, leading to distrust of the new friend. Yet nothing in the new friendship necessarily prompted a need to be distrustful. Our brain layered in a past experience to a similar experience ("friendship"), without evaluating if the current experience does in fact warrant such a reaction. If you then pull back and withhold of yourself in the new relationship as a protective strategy to avoid betrayal, you unintentionally may weaken the closeness of the friendship by not showing up as your full, authentic self. Mindful awareness allows us to peel off the brain's layers of judgment and experience the new relationship as a brand new experience, unique and happening for the first time.

Now that you have a better understanding of what we mean by mindfulness and why it is a helpful skill, we'll move into some introductory mindfulness meditation practices.

Chapter 2: It Starts with the Breath

What: Use your breath as an anchor for awareness with a beginner's mindfulness technique.

Why: The average person takes between roughly 17,000 and 23,000 breaths per day. Each breath is bringing rich information to the nervous system regarding wellness. The pace of the breath, the depth of the breath, and the "openness" of the breath (measured by dilation of the bronchial passages) are all connected to the sympathetic nervous system. When the sympathetic nervous system is activated and we enter fight or flight, our breath becomes faster and more shallow with constriction of the bronchial passages. The brain then scans the body and monitors changes, interpreting these changes as evidence of safety or lack thereof. When the brain notes shallow, rapid breathing, *even though the brain triggered this change*, the brain uses this as additional evidence that we are not safe. Tuning into our breath allows the brain to reset and settle the nervous system as we gently remind ourselves we are ok. This rapidly shuts down the fight or flight response, and moves us into parasympathetic nervous system activation (sometimes called "rest and digest").

When we practice mindfulness meditation, we use something to anchor our awareness to the present moment. Using the breath as an anchor for awareness has a unique benefit: we are always breathing. You could be anywhere, doing anything, and experiencing any emotional state, and you will also be breathing. Every breath provides a moment for connection, rich with sensory information, and a singular, unique experience.

How: Give yourself three to five minutes for this exercise, and to reap the benefits, schedule time at least daily for practice. Find a comfortable seat: in a chair, on a cushion on the floor, or even sitting up in bed with a pillow for your back. While it is certainly ok to practice meditation lying down, or to use meditation practice to help relax before bed, it's also important to find times for mindfulness meditation when we are alert and awake as we are working to train the mind to direct attention. If you are in a less-private space, it's perfectly ok to stay focused on the breath without closing your eyes; you'll just look like you are deep in thought.

Close your eyes, or let them gently defocus. Bring your awareness fully to your breath. Notice the breath as you breathe in, and as you breathe out. Don't try to control the breath in any way, but merely notice it as it is occurring. What do you notice? What is the quality of the air: warm or cool, scented, humid or dry? Where do you experience the breath in your body? Can you follow the breath on the way in: through the nasal passages, the throat, and deep into the lungs? Can you follow the exhale, from the sensation of tension when the abdomen rises to the release of air through lungs, throat, and nose or mouth? Do you experience the breath elsewhere in your body, perhaps noticing the rise and fall of shoulders, belly, or chest, or the gentle brush of the arms against the side body? Notice all the experiences of the breath. You might notice some of this verbally: "I feel the air in my nose and pressure on my diaphragm." And you might notice this at a level *beneath* words, recognizing and connecting with pure sensation. There are no rights or wrongs to this exercise, just be an observer of the breath and experience each breath as it occurs.

Your mind may wander onto other topics. That is the nature of mind. When this happens, eventually you will become aware that you are thinking about other things. This moment of awareness is where growth occurs; it is being mindful of the nature of the mind. When this happens, gently redirect your attention to your breath and let go of the other thoughts. Try not to judge yourself harshly; you are learning a new practice. The mind is used to bringing you interesting things to think about, so it is doing what it knows how to do. The observing "you" of your mind is tasked with redirecting attention to the breath. Other possible objects of focus, such as thoughts, sensations, feelings, and urges, become background music while our mind rests in the rise and fall of the breath.

If you find it easier to use a guided meditation for breath awareness, you can access a recording on my webpage, www.drkimdwyer.com/books. You will also find many recordings available online and through apps such as "Insight Timer." When you are comfortable practicing breath awareness without a recording, you might find it helpful to use a meditation timer to track an interval of time with a gentle alert. I like the timing bells on the Insight Timer app.

Reflection and Implementation Tool

My main takeaways from this chapter:

My goal to use this in my own life:

Specific opportunities I may have to use this strategy or skill:

Obstacles to using this skill and meeting this goal:

Reflection and Implementation Tool

How to problem solve these obstacles

My commitment to use this skill (rate 0-10):

After implementation, here is my reflection on how this worked for me:

Raindrop moments where I can use this skill in the future:

Chapter 3: 3 Minute Breath Reset

What: Feeling frazzled? Hit the reset button with a super-quick breath awareness meditation.

Why: Sometimes starting a new good habit is daunting. We may all have great intentions, but then life happens. That great idea of getting up early to meditate, exercise, make a healthy breakfast... it doesn't always launch seamlessly, even when we know these things will help us start the day moving in the right direction. Whatever the reason is, we can all use a quick reset to get back on course.

The good news is, you can get started with mindfulness meditation with very short periods of time. Carving out an hour to sit and meditate might be great for some, but it may not be a great fit for you. And that's ok. But more likely than not, you can find three minutes once a day to focus on your breath. Who knows? With a little practice, you might just find multiple three-minute chunks of time for breath awareness.

How: Your first step will be to identify when you might practice a three-minute breath awareness meditation. I'll give you two suggestions.

First, you might consider other things that you do for three minutes a day that don't require you to do anything but wait. Those three minutes would be a great time to fit in a breath awareness meditation. Brewing a cup of tea or coffee, heating up lunch in the microwave, waiting for a document to print, or a commercial break of a television program all come to mind. By pairing these three-minute moments that happen daily with three minutes of meditation practice, you will fit in meditation without even realizing it and without "losing" time from any other activities.

Second, you might work on recognizing the moments when you really need a three minute break. What are your own internal "red flags" indicating your stress response is flaring up? Do you notice your heart is beating fast, your cheeks are growing warm, you are raising your voice, or you are having an uptick in fatalistic thoughts? You may notice external red flags; situations that predictably trigger a stress response, such as traffic, meetings with certain coworkers, driving the school car pool lane, or the "witching hour" of homework time, dinnertime, and tired people to get ready for bed. Whatever your warning sign is, when you notice it, pat yourself on the back for having awareness and then take a three minute pause.

To practice, either close your eyes or let your eyes defocus. Without trying to control your breath, just focus on taking a breath in and then letting it go. On the in breath, silently count the breath, and on the out breath, repeat a calming word like "peace." For instance, breathe in, "one", breathe out, "peace," breathe in "two", breathe out, "peace", etc. Twenty-one breaths are approximately three minutes. If you have a mala bracelet, it most likely has twenty-one beads, which is great for tracking this practice. Alternatively, you can set a timer. Personally, I like the Insight Timer app with the availability of gentle singing bowl and meditation bell sounds as opposed to the alarm on my phone.

Repeat this at least daily to reap the benefits of a quick reset and recharge.

Reflection and Implementation Tool

My main takeaways from this chapter:

My goal to use this in my own life:

Specific opportunities I may have to use this strategy or skill:

Obstacles to using this skill and meeting this goal:

Reflection and Implementation Tool

How to problem solve these obstacles

My commitment to use this skill (rate 0-10):

After implementation, here is my reflection on how this worked for me:

Raindrop moments where I can use this skill in the future:

Chapter 4: From Breath to Habit

What: Take a breath awareness practice and make it a habit woven seamlessly throughout your day.

Why: If you're a seasoned mindfulness meditator, you've probably practiced breath awareness meditation before even opening this book. And if you're not a seasoned meditator, hopefully you started on chapter one, and, by now, have spent some time working on mindfulness of the breath. Breath awareness meditation uses the breath as an "anchor" for focused attention. This practice allows us to rest our attention on the breath, while thoughts, sensations, feelings, and urges come and go, fading into the background of our minds.

Sitting down and practicing formal meditation is wonderful. But most of us don't have the luxury of meditating all day long. For most people I know, this would not be a practical and productive way to live. We need techniques that allow us to connect with the world mindfully throughout our day. We can borrow this from a modification of a more formal breath awareness practice. In doing so, each breath is transformed into a new and unique connection to the present moment. We'll make this strategy occur more frequently and with ease by working to create a new habit.

How: Now that you've been experiencing mindfulness of the breath, our goal is to link this practice to our daily life in a way that is easy to remember and rewarding. Habits are established when we (1) have a need, (2) engage in a behavior, and then (3) experience a reward. When the reward is strong enough, it leads to a desire to repeat the behavior in the future in order to gain the reward. However, we often need a little kick in the pants to get going with a new habit, no matter the desired reward. We need help to initiate the habit. The hardest part of developing the habit of exercise is getting to the gym or putting on the running shoes. Once we are at the gym or outside with shoes on, the ensuing workout is much more likely to occur.

By connecting a new behavior to a naturally occurring behavior or situation, we can help speed up the habit cycle. Pick something that naturally occurs throughout your day. If you answer a lot of phone calls or emails at work, it could be hanging up a call or hitting 'send' on an email. If you are up and about a lot, it could be walking through a doorway. If you drive a lot, perhaps it's sitting at a red light.

Having identified your frequently occurring situation, you can now pair that situation with breath awareness for several breaths. If sending an email is your targeted habit-learning time, it might look something like this: You finish composing your email and hit send. At that moment, you gently close your eyes or allow your gaze to defocus. You bring your full attention to the next one to four breaths (depending on your time constraints). Notice everything about the breath: the sensations of the air moving through your body, the changing areas of tension or relaxation as you breathe, the motion of your shoulders, chest, and abdomen, the experience of your thoughts perhaps settling as you realign your attention to only your breath. You might try repeating a mantra or even just the word "one" with each exhale.

It takes time to nurture a new habit, as well as willpower and mental energy that can be draining at first. But, with repeated practice, you will likely feel the pleasant reward brought by a pause to refocus, bringing more balance and wisdom to your day. With regular practice combined with positive outcomes, less and less willpower is needed to initiate the act.

You might engage a gentle reminder as you work on developing the breath awareness habit; perhaps the word, "breathe," on a sticky note stuck on the edge of your computer screen, a unique bracelet you can wear as a visual reminder, or a pebble in your pocket as a tactile reminder.

Reflection and Implementation Tool

My main takeaways from this chapter:

My goal to use this in my own life:

Specific opportunities I may have to use this strategy or skill:

Obstacles to using this skill and meeting this goal:

Reflection and Implementation Tool

How to problem solve these obstacles

My commitment to use this skill (rate 0-10):

After implementation, here is my reflection on how this worked for me:

Raindrop moments where I can use this skill in the future:

Chapter 5: Get Out Of Your Space; Get Out Of Your Head

What: Mindful awareness of the outside environment.

Why: In this chapter, we'll shift our attention to sensations outside of the body to connect with the world around us. There is no better present moment connection than the second-by-second intel brought to the brain by our sensory organs, especially when we enter the rich sensory environment that is just outside of our door. Working to experience these senses fully without judging the information and without hoarding positive experiences or avoiding negative experiences, helps us to center in the moment. When we strengthen our ability to attend through these more formal, contrived practices, we have better ability to bring this non-judging attention to the rest of our lives, including those moments over which we do not have control.

In addition, being outside, especially earlier in the day, gives us a dose of sunshine which helps our internal clocks to register the day, which can aid in sleep. If you are under artificial lights all day, you'll especially want to work a quick shot of sunshine and fresh air into your daily routine. Even if it isn't particularly sunny, connecting with nature and the weather has major benefits for the health of our brains and bodies.

How: Go outside and spend 5 to 10 minutes (or longer). Practice focusing your awareness on what is around you. Notice with all five senses. Look in all directions and notice the variations in color and texture; not just "what" you see but the way the images move across your visual field. Notice everything that you hear, including close up sounds and sounds that are more distant. Feel with your whole body--the chill of breeze or warmth of sun on your skin, the feel of the ground beneath your feet, textures of handrails, benches, foliage. Observe the smells in the air and see if the air even has a taste. You might find yourself able to notice these sensations at a level below language--just pure experience. Spend five minutes being truly aware of your surroundings without judgment. When your judging mind comes in ("it's too hot/cold", "it smells like pollution", "it's beautiful out, I wish I could be out here all day") just notice the thoughts, label them as thoughts, and return your attention to your senses.

If you have more time, try taking off your shoes and socks and walking in bare feet. Experience the difference in surfaces, texture, temperature, and other sensations available when you so directly interact with the ground beneath you. How does this increase your awareness and present moment focus? Your raindrop practice of noticing the environment and your connection with nature could come at any time you have access, glancing out your window while working, driving with the car window rolled down, or taking a stroll to collect your mail.

Reflection and Implementation Tool

My main takeaways from this chapter:

My goal to use this in my own life:

Specific opportunities I may have to use this strategy or skill:

Obstacles to using this skill and meeting this goal:

Reflection and Implementation Tool

How to problem solve these obstacles

My commitment to use this skill (rate 0-10):

After implementation, here is my reflection on how this worked for me:

Raindrop moments where I can use this skill in the future:

Chapter 6: Cultivating Contentment

What: Bring intention and awareness to your experiences of contentment.

Why: Did you hear about Finland, the happiest country in the world? Guess who is not the happiest country in the world? That's right, everyone else... but the USA fell from 14th to 18th in terms of happiness (2018 rankings). The Scandinavian countries remain at the top of the 2018 list. Finland is followed by Norway (#1 previously), Denmark, and Iceland. You'd think with all that snow and cold and low light levels in winter, they wouldn't be quite so content, but you'd be wrong.

There is a concept in Scandinavian countries called "hygge," pronounced "HUE-gah". It is a Danish concept relating to the sense of contentment in life's simple pleasures. The Oxford English Dictionary defines hygge as "a quality of coziness and comfortable conviviality that engenders a feeling of contentment or well-being." Sounds like a key reason these Scandinavian countries are amongst the happiest in the world; they allow their attention and awareness to rest on the simple pleasures and rituals in life that make day-to-day living more pleasant. In my mind, this is basically mindful awareness at its best. Yes, there's a little orchestration to make sure you have the simple pleasures around you--those yummy slipper socks that you put on when you get home, a warm meal on the table, the candle that you light on your desk--but the enjoyment of these items and rituals takes root in focused attention to the present moment and not necessarily in the items themselves.

How: Examine the rituals and simple pleasures occurring throughout your day. I bet there are a lot of them that you take for granted. I do the same. We are hurried and harried and our attention is pulled in many directions. But when you slow down and focus, what are the little things that bring you great pleasure, that make your world feel gentle and cozy, and that bring you a sigh of contentment? If you're a stationary geek like I am, it's a pen that you love or a beautiful notebook in which to record your thoughts and new ideas. It could be a ritual around getting home from work

(I'm picturing Mr. Roger's switching out his blazer for the comfy cardigan in his hall closet, his work shoes for sneakers). If you work outside of your home, what rituals can you create that bring hygge to your workplace? A special memento or photo on your desk, a throw blanket or cushy pillow on your office chair, a favorite mug for morning coffee, or, my favorite, a set of gel pens that write like butter?

Try choosing two or three changes to make in your "daily space" (home or office) that bring you a sense of simple pleasure. That's just the first step, though. Once you have them in place, it's your job to bring mindful awareness to them when they enter your field of sight. Focus your attention on the way they look or feel, the memories they evoke, the desires or urges they bring up, and rest your awareness in the sense of contentment they bring. I think we could all use more hygge in our lives!

Reflection and Implementation Tool

My main takeaways from this chapter:

My goal to use this in my own life:

Specific opportunities I may have to use this strategy or skill:

Obstacles to using this skill and meeting this goal:

Reflection and Implementation Tool

How to problem solve these obstacles

My commitment to use this skill (rate 0-10):

After implementation, here is my reflection on how this worked for me:

Raindrop moments where I can use this skill in the future:

Chapter 7: Bring the Outdoors In

What: Connect to the greater world even if you're inside. Plants filter the air and connect us to the natural world.

Why: If you are like most people, you spend about 90% of your time indoors, most likely a split between your home and your office. What connects us most intimately to our environment is our breath. About fifteen times per minute--17,000 to 30,000 times a day! -- you breathe in, use what your body needs, and exhale. The complicated gas exchange that places the right levels of oxygen and carbon dioxide in your blood comes with a price: you're also breathing in any particulate matter and allergens in your environment.

Ever thought much about particulates present in your indoor air? We hear a lot about air pollution outdoors from cars and machinery, but many people don't give much thought to indoor air. Office buildings in particular can be a source of contaminated air as they are frequently closed systems (no operable windows to open for ventilation), which can even lead to something called "sick building syndrome." In addition to being harmful to your heart and respiratory system, sick building syndrome leads to drops in cognitive functioning. In other words, dirty air dulls your mind.

So, what's an indoor-dweller to do? There are fancy, and often expensive, air purifiers that can be purchased, as well as air quality sensors that will tell you about your air quality. You can also freshen your air, and brighten your spirits, with Mother Nature's air filters: plants. Not only will they help to purify your air, there is research support for plants decreasing mental fatigue and improving the sense of physical wellbeing. The reminder of nature, and of life in general, outside of your own internal world also provides a rich opportunity to practice mindful awareness.

How: Part of what NASA deems "nature's life support system," plants reduce the particulates in the air and use carbon dioxide to produce oxygen during photosynthesis. Since photosynthesis mostly occurs during the day due to the need for sunlight, while you are busy working, that plant on your desk is a little oxygen factory and a personal air filter. Microorganisms in the soil will also go to work munching on and breaking down the bad stuff present in the air.

You'll want to find a plant companion that will grow well in your indoor conditions, so consider how much sunlight your desk or kitchen counter receives as well as the presence of fluorescent lighting. If you have pets, you might also check to make sure your new plant friend is not toxic if accidentally nibbled by your fur baby. Many smaller houseplants will cost around $5 to $20 depending on the size. Love flowers? Try an African violet, moth orchid, kalanchoe, seasonal flowering cactus, or forced bulbs in a dish garden during the winter months. Got a brown thumb? Try cut flowers on your desk to bring the outside world to you.

How does this relate to mindfulness? Your plant or flowers serve as a reminder of your connection to all that is bigger than you. Each time you look at your plant, let it be a visual anchor to the ecosystem at large. Perhaps pause, reconnect to the moment, center on your breath, and acknowledge your place in the bigger world. And offer gratitude for these little plants that not only brighten our space but evolved in tandem with us to balance the chemicals in the air. In addition, caring for something other than yourself is a small expression of your interdependence with the world at large, your place in the nature of things, and your ability to show compassion towards others.

Reflection and Implementation Tool

My main takeaways from this chapter:

My goal to use this in my own life:

Specific opportunities I may have to use this strategy or skill:

Obstacles to using this skill and meeting this goal:

Reflection and Implementation Tool

How to problem solve these obstacles

My commitment to use this skill (rate 0-10):

After implementation, here is my reflection on how this worked for me:

Raindrop moments where I can use this skill in the future:

Chapter 8: Mind Your Mocha

What: Use an everyday coffee break as an opportunity to explore mindful presence.

Why: If you've been working on mindfulness practice, you may find yourself spending time in formal meditation, perhaps seated or walking, as you identify an area of present moment focus. And that's great. Formal practice opportunities provide us with skills that we can transfer to everyday life. Strengthening our "mindfulness muscle" during times of quiet helps us to bring those same skills into play when we are dealing with chaos. Think about how you might teach a child learning to ride a bike. You'd likely teach them on a quiet cul de sac and not on a four-lane parkway.

But if your practice never moves off of your meditation cushion or your mat, you may be wondering how these moments of quiet awareness help inform our day-to-day living. Working to strengthen our use of mindfulness skills when we are not formally meditating is also important, the so-called raindrop moments I'm recommending we make use of throughout the day.

The reality is, any moment is an opportunity for mindfulness practice, as long as we approach the moment with curiosity and free of judgments and preconceived notions. This is easier said than done. Our brain is an extremely well-developed pattern-finder and concept-former. We can navigate complex social and environmental situations precisely because our brain has already laid down mental tracks about what to expect and how to respond. That's a great skill, most of the time. But, when those preconceived judgments and notions about how to respond interfere with our ability to see a situation for how it actually is, or to experience that it may in fact be different from prior situations, our pattern-decoding system fails to capture the nuances of our ever-evolving lives. When such situations trigger defensive responses based on uncomfortable past experiences that do not accurately reflect our current experience, we can get in real trouble. This is a normal, understandable, habitual response based on past patterns. Mindfulness practices bring us the opportunity to notice that we are separate from our thoughts and we can reduce our attachment to unexamined thoughts.

Bringing curiosity into everyday experiences helps us practice seeing each situation for its newness and uniqueness. Mindful attention to your morning java hit or cuppa tea is one of many opportunities to experience applied mindfulness. By calling attention to a situation, you've experienced a multitude of times, likely not with your full awareness, you call on the intentional nature of directed presence.

How: Connecting with sensory experiences is the surefire way to be mindfully present. All sensory information occurs in the here-and-now. For example, if I asked you how you experience a strawberry, you'd probably tell me it's red, has green leaves, and tastes sweet. But if I handed you a strawberry and asked you to tell me your present moment experience of it, you might comment on the color being more of a ruby tone but lighter and fading to white at the stem end, with the stem being a darker-, almost bruised-, shade of green. You'd comment on the texture of the berry with its bumpy seeds, you'd notice the burst of juice and sweetness as you bit into it, and you might comment on the texture in your mouth and the sound that biting into the berry creates. To truly experience a strawberry in the present moment is far different than to recall the memory of the concept of "strawberry."

Your morning cup of coffee, tea, or other beverage of choice, is a great way to apply mindfulness practice to a very rich sensory experience. You might start by noticing everything you see: bubbles on the surface, the opacity or transparency of the fluid, the way your creamer flows into the dark liquid and changes its color, the appearance of your coffee mug, the wavering droplets of steam coming from the surface. Notice the sound of your spoon as you stir your drink.

Wrap your hands around your mug and notice the texture of the mug (is it smooth or rough?), the temperature of the mug, the weight of the mug in your hands. Now close your eyes and notice those textures and temperatures again. Did they change once your sense of touch took over?

With your eyes closed, inhale deeply. What do you notice? How do you experience the smell of your coffee or tea? Can you feel the heat in the air as you breathe it in? Our sense of smell connects almost immediately to the emotion and memory centers of our brain, so bring awareness to any feelings or memories stirred up by the aroma of your beverage.

Carefully bring your mug to your mouth and notice the heat before you take a sip, and the feeling of the mug on your lips. As you sip your drink, notice the sensations of heat, bitterness, sweetness, or flavors, and notice how those change as your drink hits different areas of your tongue. Notice how the heat changes as it cools, and notice any sounds associated with drinking your beverage.

As you practice this exercise, it is totally normal to lose your attention and realize you are thinking about things other than the sensory experiences of your drink. That's just fine, and exactly what our brains like to do. When you notice this happening, just gently lead your attention back to your coffee. Any important thoughts that come up and appear to demand your attention during this exercise will still be there and come back for your attention later.

Not a coffee or tea fan? You can bring this mindful awareness exercise to any food or beverage. Raisins and chocolate are two favorite foods for similar mindfulness exercises if coffee isn't your thing. You can even explore bringing mindful attention to eating an entire meal.

You could also bring mindful awareness to explore distinctions within categories of food; for instance, green tea versus black tea, dark roast coffee versus breakfast blend, etc. Purposefully explore these subtle distinctions.

Reflection and Implementation Tool

My main takeaways from this chapter:

My goal to use this in my own life:

Specific opportunities I may have to use this strategy or skill:

Obstacles to using this skill and meeting this goal:

Reflection and Implementation Tool

How to problem solve these obstacles

My commitment to use this skill (rate 0-10):

After implementation, here is my reflection on how this worked for me:

Raindrop moments where I can use this skill in the future:

Chapter 9: Mindful Hydration

What: Hydrate your body while enjoying a moment of mindfulness. Focus your attention, and your gratitude, towards your glass of water.

Why: All of our experiences are opportunities for mindful awareness. We have innumerable moments when we can direct our attention to the present. As we've already explored, often our easiest point of reentry to present moment experience is our senses. And what better to provide us with sensory information than a cool glass of water?

If you're like most people, you can probably use a little more water anyway. A typical suggestion is that we drink 64 ounces of water a day (or 8 glasses of 8 ounces each) ... roughly half a gallon of water. Your needs will depend on your climate, altitude, exercise level, and your body's unique needs, so of course it's best to ask your medical provider for suggestions. Regardless, use your opportunities to hydrate as a chance to practice your awareness of the present moment.

How: Pour a glass of water. Rather than drinking it while thinking of other things, direct your full attention to the glass of water and your experience of drinking it. Examine it with all five senses--what does it look like, what does the glass feel like in your hands, what is the sound of the glass filling at the tap, what is the temperature of the water and how does that change when it is in your mouth, where do you feel the water in your body as you swallow, what is the taste and smell of the water? Notice any emotions or thoughts that arise as you drink and label them (for instance, having a feeling of gratitude for fresh water, having a thought about the dirty glasses I see in the sink), and redirect your focus onto the present moment experience.

The nature of the mind is to follow those thought and emotion threads, which inevitably pull us away from the present moment. While there's nothing wrong with planning, organizing, and prioritizing, engaging in the busy activities of the mind while we are trying to focus on the present moment removes us from a state of mindful awareness. If you're going to use your time to think about dirty glasses in the sink, then a mindful and intentional approach would be to focus 100% of your attention to thinking about dirty glasses in the sink. If you're going to drink a glass of water, put 100% of your focus back to the experience of drinking water and let go of the "dirty glasses" thoughts. They will disappear on their own when you don't pay attention to those thoughts, and you can address the dishes when you are done with your water awareness meditation. (Take it from me, those dirty dishes don't just disappear because you're not thinking about them!) You can also notice those thoughts and label them "worrying thoughts," "commenting thoughts," "thoughts about lunch," etc.

The metaphor of beginner's mind is a great one to bring to your water meditation. Imagine you have never experienced a glass of water before. Perhaps you're an alien visiting earth and trying to have a full human experience. How would you experience the glass of water? You've never had this exact glass of water before, so what makes it uniquely connected to the present moment? Perhaps you'll also want to bring some gratitude meditation into your practice. Roughly 60% of an adult's body is made of water; clearly, it is a life force we cannot live without. Having easy access to clean drinking water is a true luxury that first world dwellers take for granted.

Enjoy your glass of water with gratitude and without the divided attention of multi-tasking. You'll wind up hydrated with the added benefit of a meditation break!

Reflection and Implementation Tool

My main takeaways from this chapter:

My goal to use this in my own life:

Specific opportunities I may have to use this strategy or skill:

Obstacles to using this skill and meeting this goal:

Reflection and Implementation Tool

How to problem solve these obstacles

My commitment to use this skill (rate 0-10):

After implementation, here is my reflection on how this worked for me:

Raindrop moments where I can use this skill in the future:

Chapter 10: Body Awareness

What: Your body is a direct connection to the present moment. Use it to tune in to the right-now with non-judgmental attention.

Why: My favorite definition of mindfulness is directed attention to the present moment without judgment. To me, this holds three demands:

1. Attention that you are controlling. You decide where it goes and do your best to redirect it when it wanders.

2. Present moment. We use information in the here-and-now as a focus of our attention, an anchor for the mind if you will. Here and now information typically includes external sensory information (what you hear, see, feel, smell, and taste), internal observations (our thoughts and emotions), and bodily sensations.

3. Without judgment. We are looking to strengthen a skill and notice things without labeling them and categorizing them, which are higher order cognitive/linguistic capacities. We are simply experiencing them.

I love the oft-used analogy of "beginner's mind." We can experience things right now, without judgment, as if we have never experienced them before. Because really, once we peel off the layers of judgment, expectation, and labeling, each of these experiences is actually its very own experience with its own unique qualities.

The body provides a rich source of experiences for cultivating mindful awareness. We receive information not only from our senses but also from the complex feedback systems of nerves, skeletal muscles, smooth muscles, and facial expressions. Your body sensations are always with you, allowing you to tap into this rich source of mindful practice virtually anywhere and anytime.

If you're like many people, you may have become quite good at tuning out what your body is telling you. Uncomfortable desk chair leading to pinching in your lower back? Power through, it's almost quitting time. Sensations in your throat and gut telling you that third cup of coffee was too much acid without food? Take those antacids and keep going; I need my caffeine and no time for breakfast. Mind wandering and eyes growing heavy? Keep working, it's just the afternoon slump, grab something from the snack cart.

Reading these examples, you might think they reflect a poor shepherd of one's body. Truth is, how often do we even notice these sensations when our mind is focused intensely on production and doing? We may unintentionally (mindlessly, if you will) ignore our body in pursuit of a goal. Using a body scan meditation provides us with an opportunity to bring nonjudgmental attention to the present moment, encouraging us to be a better guardian of our body's needs by recognizing change so that we can respond to it with kindness and compassion.

How: Sit or lie down in a place where you will be relatively undisturbed for a period of time. You can do this slowly and spend fifteen minutes or longer. Or you can use an abbreviated practice that will only take a few minutes. Begin by gently closing your eyes and focus on a few breath cycles, just noting the flow of air in and out of your body and letting your attention rest in your breath. Then you will shift your attention to your body, beginning with your feet and moving to the head, spending as much time as you like on each area of the body. Notice sensations: perhaps warmth or coolness, tightness, tingling, aching, comfort, dryness, relaxation. Your goal is not to change anything about your body, but just to notice it. However, many people report feeling more relaxed during this exercise, which could be just as much about tuning into the body and letting go of the mind as it is about relaxing the body.

After moving through each muscle system and limb (feet, legs, lower torso, abdomen, chest, shoulders, arms, hands, fingers, neck, face, and head), try to bring attention to the body as a whole. Working together, notice all the parts of your body that make up your physical being. Feel the unhampered flow of breath, perhaps envisioning it entering through the sole of one foot, flowing up to the crown of the head, and leaving through a reverse journey, exiting through the sole of the other foot. Notice any sticky areas where the air doesn't flow as easily, and gently bring your attention to those areas. There is no right or wrong, correct or incorrect, approach. Just notice your experience. As your mind wanders, which is the nature of mind, just gently notice and label the wandering and redirect your focus to the body.

With practice, you will likely be able to tune in to the "zone" of what's happening in your body more rapidly. When time is limited and you need a brief reset, you might practice a quick mindful body scan periodically through your day. What is my body telling me and how can I tend to my body's needs? Is this a time when I need to stretch and refuel on a healthy snack? Chat with a coworker or neighbor while breathing in some fresh air? Or sit in a patch of sunshine for a few moments? These brief, informal practices of mindfulness sprinkled through the day reconnect us with the present moment.

Reflection and Implementation Tool

My main takeaways from this chapter:

My goal to use this in my own life:

Specific opportunities I may have to use this strategy or skill:

Obstacles to using this skill and meeting this goal:

Reflection and Implementation Tool

How to problem solve these obstacles

My commitment to use this skill (rate 0-10):

After implementation, here is my reflection on how this worked for me:

Raindrop moments where I can use this skill in the future:

Chapter 11: Mindful Motion

What: Use the opportunity presented by a walk to connect fully to breath, senses, and body.

Why: How often do we move through this world, oblivious to what is around us, with our mind solely focused on our destination? We get so wrapped up in our internal dialogue and anticipating what will happen next that we miss almost everything around us, all that we see, hear, feel, smell, and taste; as well as many things within us, such as the flow of the breath, the motion of our body through space, the sensations from our muscles, the connection to and departure from the Earth with each step. A simple walk from your vehicle to your destination or from your desk to the copy machine or a colleague's office provides a rich opportunity to reset the brain through mindful connection.

Mindfulness of motion can be a planned and formal mindfulness exercise. You might decide to practice a mindful walk for a specific amount of time. This could be a walk outside, a walk around the perimeter of a large room, through a building, or around a track. The destination is not important and frankly inconsequential. The purpose is to intentionally practice noticing the experience of walking.

You might also choose to use mindfulness of motion in the "raindrop" style. Each time you are walking, you have a choice. You can choose to focus on the sensations arising from the motion of walking, or you can choose to focus on thoughts and feelings. Neither of these choices is correct or incorrect, but by intentionally selecting your focus, you are practicing mindfulness. You can also view short walks throughout the day as opportunities for a brief nervous system reset, using these moments as an opportunity for mindful awareness of your inner and outer worlds.

How: As I stated, mindfulness of motion can be practiced formally or informally. You might start by making this a formal and planned practice. To do so, select a time when you will have five to ten minutes available. Use a gentle alarm on your phone or another device (I love the Insight

Timer app for this) so that you can let go of any need to focus on time and whatever is happening later in your day.

Choose an easy route that you know, so that you can keep your attention focused entirely in the moment: perhaps around the block, around the perimeter of your office building, or even around an indoor or outdoor track. To walk mindfully, bring your attention to each step. You might feel the connection of your heel to the ground and the accompanying sensations of pressure, followed by the lift of the heel as pressure moves along the sole of the foot to the toes, followed by a pressure in the toes that propels the foot into the air as your other foot connects to the Earth. You might also focus further up the leg and notice the varying sensations of pressure in the calf and thigh muscles, noticing how this changes perhaps as the slope of the ground changes (if it does). While walking mindfully, you may also notice sensations of motion in other parts of your body, such as the gentle "swish" of your arms against your sides as they move in opposition to your legs, varying amounts of muscle tension and relaxation in your glutes and torso in response to the effort you are exerting. Also notice sensations around the head and neck that indicate motion; air flow, warmth and coolness, changes in sounds as you approach and pass their source. You might experiment with noticing these sensations as pure sensation, without labeling or narrating them at a verbal level. Perhaps you notice changes in your respiration rate and heart rate as your walk continues or increases in effort.

The mindful walk is also a great opportunity to simultaneously be aware of sensory information beyond the impact of motion resulting in muscle tension and pressure. What do you hear, see, smell, taste, feel?

All of these bits of information provide potential points of focus for present moment awareness.

Practicing a mindful walk informally doesn't differ in content, but rather in the spontaneous and untimed nature of the walk. You might pick a familiar walk such as from your desk to the coffee maker, from your family room to the kitchen, from your office to the staff lounge. When you make this journey, think of it as an opportunity, however brief, to bring your awareness to the sensations arising from within and outside of your body.

Reflection and Implementation Tool

My main takeaways from this chapter:

My goal to use this in my own life:

Specific opportunities I may have to use this strategy or skill:

Obstacles to using this skill and meeting this goal:

Reflection and Implementation Tool

How to problem solve these obstacles

My commitment to use this skill (rate 0-10):

After implementation, here is my reflection on how this worked for me:

Raindrop moments where I can use this skill in the future:

Section 2: Mindful of Thoughts and Feelings

Chapter 12: Thought Defusion

What: Notice the experience of thoughts through labeling so that you can initially notice and then un-glue from mental experience.

Why: "I think, therefore I am." If you grew up in a Western culture, you probably just brought to mind an image of Rodin's "The Thinker" sculpture. I fully admit that most of my life, I've believed my "self" took up residence behind my eyeballs somewhere inside my head. This belief allows us to become very attached to our thought processes and even to view our thought processes as evidence of reality.

Think, for a moment, of purple elephants. Of dancing orange hippopotami. Of fantastical sunflowers growing taller than buildings. My guess is you are able to imagine at least one of these unreal images, and you can probably come up with thousands of images of your own that do not exist in reality. That right there is your experiment. We can think of things that are not real. Yes, it might be very easy to separate your reality from that of a purple elephant; in other words, we easily recognize the purple elephant as a product of the mind. However, when thoughts are not fantastical images but our perceptions and interpretations of ourselves, others, and the world, we tend to have more difficulty gaining objectivity and seeing these interpretations as potentially-not-true mental activity.

Thoughts are undeniably helpful. They allow us to take a complex world and categorize it into concepts that we can easily understand. If I see a piece of furniture with a surface parallel to the floor and about two feet off the floor with extensions to the floor that provide stability, my brain quickly triggers the thought "chair." I don't have to spend time deciding what this object is and whether or not I can sit on it.

When we apply thoughts to abstractions about the nature of self, others, and the world, we also save time and can quickly make decisions without becoming bogged down. Most of the time, these thoughts are helpful. If I have a thought of myself as someone who doesn't enjoy taking risks or the sensation of motion, I'm probably going to quickly decide not to spend a Saturday at the amusement park (true story). Avoiding motion sickness is generally helpful to my wellbeing. But, what if I apply this too broadly and make a snap appraisal that going to any crowded social event is "risky" and decline an invitation? Perhaps I've missed an opportunity for fun, for business networking, and to prove that I can manage an initially uncomfortable situation and still have an enjoyable evening.

Noticing thoughts as thoughts and only thoughts is the first step in gaining the distance and objectivity that we need to appraise and change thoughts. When we accept thoughts as reality, we are fused or glued to those ideas. We don't question them or their veracity, and treat them as reliable, "real" information. I like to think of these thoughts as trains coming into a station. We stand on the platform and the train comes through. The conductor reaches out and grabs us and we are off on that thought-train ride without even a decision point about whether this train of thought is helpful to us or not, or whether we even want to ride that train. This is thought fusion. We are identified with our thoughts and do not question them or view them as existing separate from ourselves.

When we can stop for the briefest of moments and notice a thought as just that, a thought, which is potentially true or untrue, helpful or unhelpful, we are being mindful of the nature of thought. This is often referred to as thought defusion; untethering yourself from your thoughts. It's standing on the platform, watching the train come into the station, and saying "hey, that's the thought train that says I hate risky situations and I should avoid them. Hmmmm, I know that train and I've ridden it before. I'm going to watch that train and decide if I feel like riding it today, or if maybe there is a different thought train that suits me better."

How: Mindfulness of thoughts can be practiced formally, like other mindfulness meditation practices. It involves sitting quietly and bringing your focus to your thoughts. Just as mindfulness of the breath uses the act of breathing as an anchor for mental awareness and focus, mindfulness of thoughts uses thought as an anchor of focus. The goal is to pay attention to thoughts and notice them simply as thoughts. The key though is to notice them but not to engage with them. You might do this by labeling them: "I'm having a thought about lunch." "I'm having a thought about my coworker irritating me." "I'm noticing thoughts about needing to get my kids started on their homework." "I'm noticing judging thoughts about my ability to do this meditation."

As you notice each thought, gently release it. If I struggle to do this, I like to use imagery. My favorite is to place a soap bubble around the thoughts and watch them drift up to the sky. A popular meditation involves placing thoughts on a leaf, placing the leaves in a stream, and watching them drift away. You'll find lots of pre-recorded "leaves on a stream" meditations if you do a quick search, and can also access recorded meditations on my website.

Once you become more aware of the nature of thought and get used to the idea that you don't have to engage with every thought, you can work to pull this technique into your daily life, raindrop style. When your brain starts stewing or spiraling on thoughts, you might take a half step away from your thoughts and just acknowledge them. "Having thoughts about...." "Getting stuck on thoughts of...." "Oh, I know this thought! It's the thought about...." Then, you choose. Do you want to think about that thought? If you do, go for it. If the thought is not helpful, truthful, or how you want to spend your time at the moment, just notice the thought and gently release it.

Reflection and Implementation Tool

My main takeaways from this chapter:

My goal to use this in my own life:

Specific opportunities I may have to use this strategy or skill:

Obstacles to using this skill and meeting this goal:

Reflection and Implementation Tool

How to problem solve these obstacles

My commitment to use this skill (rate 0-10):

After implementation, here is my reflection on how this worked for me:

Raindrop moments where I can use this skill in the future:

Chapter 13: Notice Your Thought Filters

What: Schemas help us make sense of the world, but they also lead to thinking errors when over applied.

Why: There's a lot of information in our world. Ever think what it must be like to be a newborn, trying to make sense of everything there is to see, do, hear, feel, touch, and taste in our environment? Totally overwhelming. No wonder they sleep so much. And no wonder we have such rapid growth of the brain in the first few years of life.

To make sense of our world, our brains do a great job of categorizing information. We do this with physical items in our world. I described this in the previous chapter with reference to the concept of a chair. Psychologists call these "schemas." We can then accommodate our schemas to meet new information: a swivel office chair on a 5-pronged base with wheels and a single support that holds up the seat rather than four legs? Yep, that can fit into our chair schema, and we then change the schema to reflect "elevated by a support" rather than elevated by four legs.

We make schemas all the time. And most of them are probably made in early childhood. And while a "chair" schema may seem obvious, helpful, and unlikely to be challenged in the future, other schemas are more subtle and intangible. We have schemas for types of people: parents, siblings, friends, co-workers, significant others. Those schemas include all the ways they are "supposed to" act, respond, and treat us. While it might be relatively easy to change the "chair" schema to accommodate a unique modern-art-museum-worthy chair, it might be a little more difficult to change the "friend" schema to make sense of a friend who has, for example, betrayed our trust.

The problem is, we apply these schemas almost instantaneously. Information comes in and our brain filters it through past experiences and categories. When it's appropriate (Hey, that's also a chair, go sit on it.), great. But we can also over apply our schemas and make mistakes. There are times when it is not appropriate. For instance, a person fitting your "friend" schema does something similar to something a former friend did to you in the past which was hurtful, and now you feel angry and betrayed. Yet, there might be a crucial difference in these two friends' actions. Without being mindful of the brain's over-application of schemas, we can make all kinds of errors, misperceive a person's intentions, or over personalize their actions.

To top it off, our brain has something called confirmatory bias. This means we tend to seek out information that agrees with our preconceived ideas about the world. If we have a schema that people at the grocery store are rude and inconsiderate, we will notice each time we get bumped, cut in front of, or glared at while doing the weekly shopping. We will not pay as much attention to the person who offers to let us go ahead of them in line, the person who moves their cart out of our way, or the people who smile as they pass us.

But we are not helpless souls trapped in a time-saving brain that sacrifices accuracy for speed. We can change the focus of our attention by practicing mindfulness of our thoughts.

How: Understanding how you are filtering new experiences through the conceptual framework of schemas requires getting clear on your thought processes. As such, this is the perfect situation to apply mindfulness of thought techniques and explore if you are reacting to the reality in front of you, or to your brain's imagined reality based on prior experiences.

You can use your emotional response as a warning system that perhaps you've over applied a schema. Often, when we have very strong negative emotions, it is a sign that we are responding to MORE than the situation in front of us. Yes, what is happening might be mildly irritating, frustrating, or upsetting. But a strong reaction of intense irritation, frustration, or grief could signal that we are applying a preset understanding and reaction based on a different experience (or, likely, series of experiences). For instance, harkening back to an example I used in the first chapter of this book, a slammed car door in the middle of the night that results in rage towards inconsiderate neighbors is likely a response based on more than just being awoken one specific time.

Once you have identified the possibility that you are reacting to a schema and not to your reality, you can stop and apply mindfulness techniques to examine the situation. I liken it to thinking like a scientist. What is the evidence in front of you? Try to peel away any layers of judgment, preconception, or categorical thinking, and just see the situation for what it presents right now, in your present moment awareness.

Formal meditation on thought, in which you bring awareness to the nature of your thoughts without pondering them, helps us evaluate these situations. Examine the thoughts with curiosity and release them. See what thoughts are truly connected to your present experience, and which are your brain trying to save time by rapidly, and maybe incorrectly, applying categorical thinking strategies.

To apply this strategy "raindrop style," you might pause frequently, especially when you notice a strong emotional reaction. Check in with your thoughts and feelings in these moments, and assess if your reaction (thoughts, feelings, and urges to act) matches your current situation. Conversely, are these reactions triggered by past situations and anticipated outcomes? You can modify or expand upon your mind's initial judgments when provided additional time to intentionally consider the present moment data.

Is it possible that your reaction is bigger because it truly reflects your reality? Maybe it's not the first time this particular situation has occurred. That's important information. Even so, reacting based on multiple past situations is still probably not the most helpful in the present moment. Distilling your current situation down into what is happening now will allow you to problem solve and communicate based on your present reality, and not overreact based on past situations and slights. Try using those moments of intense emotional reaction to bring mindful awareness to your situation, peeling off judgments, and noticing exactly what is happening before reacting.

Reflection and Implementation Tool

My main takeaways from this chapter:

My goal to use this in my own life:

Specific opportunities I may have to use this strategy or skill:

Obstacles to using this skill and meeting this goal:

Reflection and Implementation Tool

How to problem solve these obstacles

My commitment to use this skill (rate 0-10):

After implementation, here is my reflection on how this worked for me:

Raindrop moments where I can use this skill in the future:

Chapter 14: Mindful of the Mind's Journeys

What: Notice the trips your mind takes and the nature of your thoughts. What becomes familiar is what you will seek out.

Why: The places to which we mentally escape have a lot of power over our day. Ever find yourself moseying along and something triggers a negative thought, which triggers another negative thought, and soon you are stewing in negativity? Perhaps you begin having an imagined argument in your head with someone. The unfortunate news is that despite this being imagined, you feel the anger, and your body responds in kind with increased heart rate and muscle tension. The physical activation is real, even though the argument is about an imagined future scenario that may never occur! Silly humans, why do we do this to ourselves?

A problem with visits to negative-thought-land is this: our brain tends to seek out the familiar, and look for opportunities to confirm our beliefs. It doesn't matter if those beliefs are real or faulty, based on reality, fantasy, or imagined worst-case scenarios. If we spend a whole lot of time thinking about red Ferraris, we're likely to see a red Ferrari soon when we are out driving in our world (sounds crazy, right?). This is known as the frequency illusion or the recency illusion, sometimes referred to as the Baader-Meinhof phenomenon. (This was dubbed Baader-Meinhof by a journalist who heard of the 1970s Baader-Meinhof terrorist group for the first time, then heard of them again within the same day.)

Here's how this works: your brain learns something new or ponders something new. Selective attention then occurs, such that your brain seeks out examples and gives them more relevance or weight if they agree with your recently learned information (this is confirmatory bias). Put it together and you'll understand that if your brain is excited about something negative and you reinforce this by thinking about these negative thoughts, your brain is going to seek out more opportunities to find the negative and ponder the negative.

Fortunately, we don't have to do this anymore. As we continue to bring nonjudgmental attention to the nature of our thoughts, we can objectively notice where they tend to lead. We can watch those thoughts with curiosity rather than jumping into the water with them and swimming around for a bit. Sit on the shore and watch, rather than immersing yourself, and decide if those thoughts will be helpful today.

How: As you use formal or informal mindfulness strategies to notice your thoughts, try this: imagine your thoughts entering your head on a conveyor belt. Maybe they are sitting on the belt and traveling through your mental space, maybe they are in boxes. Whatever image seems to work for you, you can notice the thoughts and watch them keep moving. Maybe you can start to sort and label the thoughts. You're not judging them or yourself for having them, you are simply labeling them. For instance: thought about blueberry muffins, thought about neighbor's dog barking, thought about work project, thought about argument with spouse, thought about chicken noodle soup, thought about red Ferraris. (Yes, I just did that.) No need to engage with the thoughts or to swim around in the emotions or judgments that they tend to elicit. Just notice them and label them. If they are in boxes on the conveyor belt, perhaps you have a giant stamp you use to label them, then seal them up and watch them travel away from you.

To practice mindfulness of thoughts in a less formal setting, you might use your physiological and behavioral cues to let you know when increased attention to thought would be in your best interest. What are your warning signs that you are getting sucked into a negative thought spiral? Does your heart rate go up? Do you reach for a donut? Do you start imagining venting to a friend? Do you start rehearsing mental arguments? Do your shoulders start gravitating closer to your ears?

Whatever your signs are, let those become your red flags. Notice these signs and break the cycle. You might tell yourself to stop (aloud or silently). Maybe envision being at a crossroads with a big stop sign in front of you and some choices of which path to take. Rather than the familiar path into negative thoughts, consider watching those thoughts and choosing to take a different path. Every negative cue is a raindrop opportunity to bring awareness to the present moment.

Negative thoughts are frequently triggered by something negative. Go figure! Not getting caught in negative thoughts is not a suggestion to ignore anything negative in your life. But it is a suggestion to notice and choose whether dwelling in the negative will serve you well. If it won't, then don't dwell there. But if there's a problem to be solved, by all means, solve it. Have the difficult conversation or work through whatever needs to be understood.

But do it in real life, not in your head. Arguments with yourself don't help anyone.

Reflection and Implementation Tool

My main takeaways from this chapter:

My goal to use this in my own life:

Specific opportunities I may have to use this strategy or skill:

Obstacles to using this skill and meeting this goal:

Reflection and Implementation Tool

How to problem solve these obstacles

....

....

....

My commitment to use this skill (rate 0-10):

....

....

....

After implementation, here is my reflection on how this worked for me:

....

....

....

Raindrop moments where I can use this skill in the future:

....

....

....

Chapter 15: Mindful When the Mind is Full

What: Create space for mindfulness even when the mind is worried.

Why: When you think of mindfulness meditation, do you think of a sole meditator, seated on a serene mountain top, bliss and peace radiating from an enlightened face? Well, here's the deal. Just because you meditate, you are not promised bliss and peace. In fact, many seasoned meditation teachers would be quick to tell you that seeking bliss and peace is NOT the goal of mindfulness meditation. The goal is to learn to strengthen attention and to direct one's attention to the present moment, without judgment. The judgment is a big part of what leads to trouble--it becomes the mind's narrative. "Seeking bliss and peace" is inherently judgmental, as we are ranking a certain human experience as better than others. When we switch to a goal of being an astute observer of the present moment, bliss may be a by-product, but it is certainly not a guarantee or the destination.

We need mindfulness practices the most when our brain is overloaded. When our worries get triggered and move into overdrive, it can be very difficult, but so necessary, to connect back to the present moment. Anxiety and worry tend to be almost exclusively future tense. We worry when anticipating things that might happen in the future. In those worried moments, it can be effective to direct our focus back to the present moment. Unless we are in an acutely stressful situation in the present moment, we are probably okay. From a biological standpoint, if your life is not immediately threatened, and you are breathing and your heart is beating, you check all the "ok" boxes. Sometimes the brain needs a reminder of this simple fact; everything else is gravy.

How: Come back to the present moment when you find your mind is full of worry or you are ruminating about a problem. Our brains are amazing categorizers of information and predictors of future occurrences. When we get caught in a state of worrying, it is actually our brain's attempt to problem solve run amok. It's ok to worry, but when you're going to worry, give worry your complete attention. Better yet, call it problem solving and designate a time to problem solve.

When you're focused on a task or doing work, allow your current project have your complete attention. You might try the following exercise when worries are interfering with your focus on the task at hand.

Breathe and recenter yourself on awareness of the breath. Notice your mind's tendency to worry. You might say to yourself gently, with no judgment, "Worrying now." Reframe this as your brain's attempt to problem solve. You might say to yourself, "Thank you, brain, for trying to keep me safe by problem solving. But right now, I'm ok. Right now, I'm not problem solving, but I'll come back to this later."

Next, grab a scrap of paper and jot down the problem that you need to solve. Make an appointment with yourself to do this later--set a specific and time-limited period for problem solving, for instance, 3:00 to 3:15pm. Return your focus to your project, and try to bring full awareness to whatever it is you're doing. If you're washing dishes, notice the temperature of the water, the smell of the soap, the fizzing sound of the bubbles, the slipperiness of the dishes between your fingers, the texture of the sponge. If you're working on a project, allow yourself to immerse fully in the sensory stimuli of the environment: everything you see, hear, smell, feel, and even taste.

When it's worry time, or rather, problem solving time, be productive about it and allow your entire focus to move to your problem solving.

The difference between problem solving and worrying is that when you are problem solving, you are actively involved in finding a solution, rather than being a passive bystander while your mind hijacks a portion of your mental capacity to present you with all the worst-case scenarios. You may quickly find that the problem cannot be solved: perhaps you are missing some crucial information. If that's the case, you'll have to resolve to leave it alone until you have enough information. If you do have the info, you might try using whatever problem-solving strategies work best: a cost analysis, listing pros and cons, listing risks and advantages, consultation with others... whatever works for you to solve the problem.

Reflection and Implementation Tool

My main takeaways from this chapter:

My goal to use this in my own life:

Specific opportunities I may have to use this strategy or skill:

Obstacles to using this skill and meeting this goal:

Reflection and Implementation Tool

How to problem solve these obstacles

My commitment to use this skill (rate 0-10):

After implementation, here is my reflection on how this worked for me:

Raindrop moments where I can use this skill in the future:

Chapter 16: Mindful Focus

What: Increase focus by minimizing distractions and limiting your focus to one task at a time.

Why: We live in an increasingly distracting world. If much of your work takes place in front of a computer or with a smartphone in hand, you know too well how easy it is to lose focus. Personally, I find about half the time I sit down at my computer to work on something, I catch myself going down a rabbit hole of email responding, social media, or online shopping before I realize that I'm not working on what I intended to work on. And sometimes I can't even remember what it was I sat down to do!

Distractions take away time from the task at hand, resulting in more time needed to finish that task. But, did you know that distractions also decrease the overall quality of the work? Researchers at George Mason University studied the impact of interruptions during the planning and productivity phases of an essay writing task, chosen because this work mirrors the planning and production in many creative thought tasks. Essays written in either of the interrupted conditions were graded as significantly weaker. In a follow up experiment, they found that 96% of participants scored worse in the interrupted condition than in a non-interrupted condition.

While a windows operating system may be great on your computer with multiple tabs open at any time, your brain does not function this way. Working memory, the capacity to "hold on to information" to use for problem solving and higher order reasoning, is a finite resource. If you exceed your brain's working memory span, you can no longer attend to multiple pieces of information at the same time. Having to then recall forgotten chunks of information will, at best, slow you down, or, at worst, lead to significantly reduced production and quality of work.

How: What is a mindful worker in a multi-tasking world to do? Mindfulness is about learning to focus one's attention to the present moment without judgment. Formal mindfulness meditation practice works to hone the brain's capacity to pay attention to stimuli occurring "right now"--whether that be to the breath, to sensations in the body, to environmental stimuli, or to internal stimuli. Meditation will help to strengthen your ability to focus. You can bring these skills to use informally throughout your day, especially on projects that may be less engaging than "preferred" (read, distracting) activities.

One great informal way to work on increased focus on work is often called the Pomodoro Method. Pomodoro is Italian for tomato, and this method takes its name from the tomato shaped kitchen timers found in many kitchens. The idea is to use a timer to direct your focus for a specified time period. While you can do this old-school with a kitchen timer, you can also find apps and web pages that will time you, alerting you when you've reached your time goal, and allowing you to schedule in predetermined break periods.

You might initially select a project you'd like to complete and determine how much time you would likely need to spend in the planning phases and in the work completion phase. You might decide you need to spend an hour collecting information and organizing material for an article, and an additional hour to write the article. If you do a great job staying focused for an hour and your job is one in which you can reliably be left to do your work without interruptions, you could set your timer for an hour and make a deal with yourself not to do anything else during that time. In this way, you can spend an hour planning, take a break or work on a different task for a short time, and then return and spend an hour writing.

However, if you need to respond to things on the fly or you are often interrupted, you might wish to choose shorter time periods, like 20 or 30 minutes. Disengage from other work, if at all possible, by silencing your phone, closing any internet browsers and notifications of email or social media, and close your office door. Put a please do not disturb sign on your cubicle, or let a small group of people in your orbit know that you are not available except for true emergencies. If you find that you struggle to stay focused for the time you have allotted, shorten the time and then work to gradually increase your focus time in the future. String together multiple shorter chunks with five-minute breaks interspersed between them, and you'll finish before you know it without distractions eroding your creative process and attention. Notice your mind wandering? Those moments of noticing represent mindful awareness of the tendencies of the mind. Just notice them, perhaps label them ("mind wandering now"), and gently redirect your attention to the task at hand.

Reflection and Implementation Tool

My main takeaways from this chapter:

My goal to use this in my own life:

Specific opportunities I may have to use this strategy or skill:

Obstacles to using this skill and meeting this goal:

Reflection and Implementation Tool

How to problem solve these obstacles

My commitment to use this skill (rate 0-10):

After implementation, here is my reflection on how this worked for me:

Raindrop moments where I can use this skill in the future:

Chapter 17: Mind the Time

What: Direct mindful awareness towards your relationship with time.

Why: We spend a lot of time on time, don't we? How frequently is your day punctuated by thoughts about time and its associated constructs such as being on time, being late, and managing your time wisely? For most of us, time is always on our minds. Just look at how we talk about time: don't waste time, a stitch in time saves nine, mind the time, save time, give me more time. You'd almost think time was something to be saved in a bottle, à la the 1973 Jim Croce song.

What exactly is time? Time, and certainly the importance we give it and adherence to the rules we've created for it, is a human construct. We can measure time by the rotation of the earth, an actual observable event, but seconds, minutes, and hours are human constructs. The importance that we give to time is all on us humans.

If I had to bet, I'd put money on the fact that time-related stress often enters your life as an uninvited guest. When we are working to be as efficient as possible, it is easy for one thing to not go quite as planned. A traffic jam or car trouble, a child who does not cooperate with getting ready for school or summer camp, or a doctor's appointment that takes longer than expected all lead to lateness. Suddenly we're in Stress Central Station trying to figure out how to make up time. All of this pushes us into a zone of living where we are not likely at our best. By applying mindfulness to time, I'm inviting you to consider an alternative.

How: This week, bring your awareness to your relationship with time. You might start with a simple exercise. You'll need a stopwatch and about ten minutes of time. First, we'll work on increasing awareness of the passage of time to become a better predictor of time. Get comfortable, close your eyes, and start the time on your stopwatch. Your goal is to predict a minute. When you feel like a minute has passed, stop the stopwatch and open your eyes. Were you close? If so, great. Try a lengthier period of time, like two or three minutes. While practicing your prediction, be aware of the nature of your thoughts, the tendency of thoughts to wander, and feelings such as excitement or boredom that arise in your body, etc. If you were less accurate at predicting a minute, try it a few more times to see if you improve your skill.

Next, use about five minutes to be aware of what happens when you exist in a space outside of time. Set an alarm or a meditation countdown timer for five minutes. Get comfortable, close your eyes, and bring mindful awareness to sensations in your body, your breath, and/or your thoughts. Just notice your experience of being, making every attempt to let go of any awareness of or concerns about time. If you notice such thoughts, you might simply label them "thoughts about time" and let them go.

What happens when you operate in this space outside of time, bringing curiosity to the present moment? My guess is your stress level decreases and you gain some insight into your relationship with time. Of course, deadlines, timelines, and appointment times are necessary facts of life in our world. But we don't have to mindlessly be managed by time when we can thoughtfully approach our relationship to time.

You might continue to bring your awareness to your relationship with time by being mindful of the emotions that arise in you around time-related events, and the thoughts that accompany those emotions. Listen to the way that you talk about time and be mindful of how long "just one more minute" really lasts. One of my children gave me a major wakeup call many years ago when I told him I'd get him a snack "in just a second" and he responded with "but a second is a really long time." Not my best parenting moment, but an eye-opening one!

Reflection and Implementation Tool

My main takeaways from this chapter:

My goal to use this in my own life:

Specific opportunities I may have to use this strategy or skill:

Obstacles to using this skill and meeting this goal:

Reflection and Implementation Tool

How to problem solve these obstacles

My commitment to use this skill (rate 0-10):

After implementation, here is my reflection on how this worked for me:

Raindrop moments where I can use this skill in the future:

Chapter 18: Turn Towards Joy

What: Find the moments of joy that punctuate your day and give them your full attention.

Why: Negativity. It's all around us. Just the word feels heavy to me. Complaints. Aches and pains. Pollution. Anger. Grief. Lost opportunities. Poverty. Crime. Feeling the weight yet? Ever wonder why we give so much weight to the negatives and not to the positives?

From an evolutionary, biological standpoint, our main purpose for being here is to survive to adulthood and pass along our genetic material to our young. Yes, I do have other purposes in my life and I know that you do, too. But our physical bodies are uniquely designed for survival based on millennia of evolution starting with pre-mammalian species. Our brain has a lot of tricks to keep us alive and kicking, most of which originate in our limbic system and sympathetic nervous system. Our limbic system, and the amygdalae in particular, serves as the home base for emotion processing. We quickly assess a situation and pull out sensory information that is processed and "coded" into emotional sensations. When those emotions are of the fear-danger-anxiety variety, the body kicks the sympathetic nervous system into high gear, best known for its fight or flight response. The fight or flight response expends a lot of energy solely to keep the body safe in the face of danger. And to keep us safe in the future, the brain codes extra "valence", or importance, into memories of perceived unsafe situations, leading to further aversion of risk in the future.

Examples of true biological necessity might be a life-or-death situation. For instance, you get too close to the edge of a cliff while camping and feel the pebbles and earth start to crumble under your feet. You jump back to safety, fueled by that burst of adrenaline from your sympathetic nervous system's fight or flight response. Your brain codes in capital letters with fluorescent yellow highlighter "stay away from cliffs!" Your brain probably codes that with multiple "routes" to the information and with tons of saliency so you don't make that mistake again. Message received, thank you brain. Got it, no more cliffs.

Trouble is, our brain does this to non-physical threats. Take the snarky coworker in the break room. The rude message on social media. The person at the grocery store who is oblivious to the fact they are taking up the whole aisle. The fellow dog walker who doesn't clean up after Spot. While you may not have a full-on fight or flight response, you can bet your brain is paying attention to these negative aspects of your day, and giving them probably more weight than they need, and more weight than you want them to have. To fight these off, we have to consciously and intentionally turn towards joy.

How: The "how" for this exercise is an easy one. However, easy to do doesn't necessarily mean it's easy to remember to do. Remember, I used the word "intentional." If we want to change our relationship with the world around us so that we can change our internal representation and appraisals of the world around us, we need to bring conscious intentionality to task. We have to deliberately choose to be mindfully aware of the joy, the beauty, the kindness, and the connections around us.

It might start with paying better attention. Do you go into autopilot on your drive home from work, rehashing the work day gains and losses, practicing tomorrow's pitch or planning your work wardrobe, your dinner, or how to support your kids with homework time? Is this an opportunity to bring more attention to the present? Your work day is over, you're not cooking dinner or doing homework yet, and you have the whole evening to plan your wardrobe and approach for the next day. Can you bring mindful awareness to what you see around you on your drive home? I'm blessed to live in an area where my drive home routinely brings me views of snow-capped mountains, a drive past a reservoir that reflects trees and is frequently home to ducks and geese, and, depending on the time of the day, a westwardly drive home that often includes skies blazed orange with the sunset. I used to live in a super rural area where I could mark my drive home by the seasons; snow frosted trees in winter, redbuds in spring, tall grasses growing progressively golden over the summer, and an old broken-down barn that threatened to fall over. After two years of watching it on my 50-mile work drive, one day that barn was just a pile of boards after its presumed collapse. That was an exciting drive!

My point is, whatever your drive brings you, or whatever your moments throughout the day bring you, you can almost always find something to focus on that brings joy; that doesn't negate the fact that there are difficult times in life, lots of them, in fact. But the two states are not mutually exclusive. You do not have to be totally mired in joylessness because something is not going well. You can struggle with a child's temper tantrum AND notice that the slant of the light through your window is hitting the kitchen counter and turning it aglow. You can realize that no one put paper in the copy machine again AND enjoy the smell of freshly brewed coffee in the work room. You can lament the increased traffic in your area AND bop along to a favorite song on the radio. You can stand in line for a very long time due to the checker needing to call for a price check, AND notice the pretty floral pattern on the checker's shirt.

How can you find those moments of joy? Turn towards them, appreciate them, and let your attention rest on them, however briefly.

Reflection and Implementation Tool

My main takeaways from this chapter:

My goal to use this in my own life:

Specific opportunities I may have to use this strategy or skill:

Obstacles to using this skill and meeting this goal:

Reflection and Implementation Tool

How to problem solve these obstacles

....

....

....

My commitment to use this skill (rate 0-10):

....

....

....

After implementation, here is my reflection on how this worked for me:

....

....

....

Raindrop moments where I can use this skill in the future:

....

....

....

Chapter 19: Turning Towards Discomfort

What: Rather than avoiding discomfort, turn mindful awareness towards those things that are uncomfortable.

Why: Inevitably, life sometimes hands us lemons. There are the small lemons (kind of like key limes) and there are the great big Meyer's lemons, delivered by the crate full. I'm not going to sit here and tell you to take lemons and make lemonade. As the saying goes, you'd better also have a whole lot of sugar and water or that lemonade is not going to taste good!

I'm actually going to suggest the opposite. Rather than taking life's lemons and sweetening them, what happens when you turn towards them and really inhabit the sour for a while?

We do a really good job in Western cultures at turning away from discomfort. We deny, we squash down, we avoid. We do it through distraction. We do it through a whole host of behaviors that give our brain bursts of soothing neurochemicals and move us away from uncomfortable emotional states; behaviors such as substance use, shopping, eating, sex, getting lost in electronics or other distractions. We are not well versed in turning towards our discomfort.

I believe firmly that our emotions, the positive ones and the negative ones, exist to provide us with information. Unlike our senses, which bring in present moment information from the outside world, our emotions present us with information about our internal world. Sometimes, these emotions are not the ones we desire: fear, anxiety, stress, disappointment, sadness, grief. The experience is not comfortable, and we might try to avoid them. We may have received messages, overt and subtle, across our lifespans that we should avoid those emotions and we "don't have to feel that way." Well, we don't... yet, we might choose to feel them, because those emotions are telling us about the things that are the most dear to our very cores. If you can sit with the feeling and embrace it, you might learn something about your value system, which can then inform your actions based on wisdom.

How: Be aware this week of negative feeling states. Perhaps you initially just bring your attention to these feelings, scanning your body for where the feelings hang out, and listening to the soundtrack of thoughts associated with your feelings. You might also notice any urges that arise associated with these feelings. Urges to engage in avoidance or distraction behaviors are not uncommon when we feel uncomfortable. Acknowledge the urge ("I'm having an urge to stop thinking about this, to watch television, to eat a big bowl of ice cream") and then return to noticing your emotions and thoughts. See what happens and what presents to you over time as you stay with the uncomfortable emotion without acting on it. You can do this informally in a moment of reflection, or through a formal meditative practice.

You might notice how these feelings change over time, and how they reflect on your value system. When we can notice and sit with our feelings, mining them for information about our deeper self and core values, we can use that information to act intentionally and authentically. Without that information, we are prone to being reactive or avoiding; popping off at the roommate who leaves dirty dishes in the sink, or going on a shopping spree to cheer ourselves up after a fight with a loved one. Sitting with uncomfortable feelings in both of these instances could lead to more authentic action such as a respectful conversation about cleaning up, or a follow up conversation to reconcile.

Sitting with feelings may also lead to the realization that some of our feelings, especially anger, can be ego-driven and not reflective of our soul's deepest longings. Traffic related emotions are a good example. The irritation you may feel at a driver who cuts you off, honks their horn, or otherwise "behaves badly" may not be something that needs any kind of reaction, but simply an acknowledgement that people make mistakes and it's not in our best interest to personalize those mistakes.

This week, use negative feeling states as an opportunity to step outside of the frame of your life and observe. Turning towards these emotions, try to uncover what exactly bothered you. This could be the surface level "story" of what happened, or something deeper. Sit with these feelings and truly listen to what they are telling you about yourself and your relationship with the world around you.

Reflection and Implementation Tool

My main takeaways from this chapter:

My goal to use this in my own life:

Specific opportunities I may have to use this strategy or skill:

Obstacles to using this skill and meeting this goal:

Reflection and Implementation Tool

How to problem solve these obstacles

My commitment to use this skill (rate 0-10):

After implementation, here is my reflection on how this worked for me:

Raindrop moments where I can use this skill in the future:

Chapter 20: Inhabiting Disruption

What: Build on turning towards uncomfortable emotions by getting comfortable, fully inhabiting the uncomfortable phases of life.

Why: How often are we going about our lives, thinking things are possibly going according to plan, when we are met with disruption? Disruption--even the word sounds violent. In the face of disruption, most of us fight back. Our sense of justice rallies and we wage war against the unfairness of the situation. We think of the "could've, would've, should've" of the situation. If we had just done that one thing differently, this dreaded outcome wouldn't have happened. With egos operating under the illusion of control, we really don't like these disruptions.

I will spare you the minute details of one of my bigger disruptions in recent times, but share the major gist of it: a car accident, caused by someone else, leaving my car a total loss, myself and one of my small people needing treatment for (thankfully minor) injuries for five months. I found myself having to purchase a car on very short notice, and grieving the injustice of "I didn't do anything to cause this." As I said, thankfully the injuries healed, the car was replaced, and the distress caused by managing the accident has begun to fade from my consciousness.

But man, don't go back in time and tell me that it will all be ok. I was M-A-D. And guess what? I allowed that emotion to inform my thoughts and actions. I moved into the madness and sense of injustice, and I lived there for a good chunk of time. I felt sorry for myself, exploded at those around me who "didn't get it" and tried to make me feel better, and, legitimately, was in physical pain (likely worsened by my overall high stress level).

You've got your own stories of disruption. We all do, and many of them are far more serious and permanent than my most recent one. Jobs lost, relationships damaged and ended, illness, change, death, grief. Not to mention the infinite number of minor disruptions–the child home sick, changing our plans for the day, the interruption of a work task by an unexpected crisis, the household appliance that breaks down and sucks up our "fun money" to fix or replace it. Why do we fight disruption so much when it seems to be the norm?

In western, Judeo-Christian culture, we hold tight to what cognitive psychologists refer to as the "just world belief." This is easily summed up as "bad things happen to bad people; good things happen to good people." This is at the crux of our court system and deeply entrenched in our sense of justice. It propels the American Dream that by working hard we can pull ourselves up by our bootstraps, and it allows us to turn a blind eye to those who are marginalized, victimized, and otherwise damaged by society. Consciously or subconsciously, if something bad happens to someone, they must have done something bad to cause it, our brain reasons. In a way it is protective; our psyche can say "well that won't happen to me. I'm safe, because I don't (insert assumed transgression here). I don't drink and drive. I don't hang out in places like that. I don't wear skirts that are too short. I don't drive a red sports car… whatever rationalization is needed.

When the truly bad happens for no reason at all, this "just world" belief falls apart. We may still cling to it and try to find reasons why the bad thing happened. Maybe we didn't do something quite right and this is our payback, maybe what happened isn't "all bad" and we try to find some good in it. Because letting go of the just world belief means we have to accept that random crappy things happen, and you and I have absolutely no control over them. The car accident. The lost job. The failed relationship. The cancer diagnosis. The unthinkable loss of a dear one.

In Eastern philosophies such as Buddhism, impermanence is a central concept. Accepting that everything changes allows one to let go of earthly attachments. When we hold tight to what is no longer, we hold onto a pain that does not necessarily serve us in the moment, and we "write our future" with our past loss. While non-attachment sounds good to me in theory, it isn't so easy for me to practice. I readily admit, I fight it. I'm getting better at recognizing it though, and I think a lot of that has to do with turning towards the disruption and not away from it.

How: Rather than turning away and rallying against disruption, allow yourself to move into and inhabit the space. The disruptions referred to could be small such as the interruption by a child who wants to play while you work, or the interruption of a work call while you are trying to relax. These are great disruptions to use for practicing a new response, perhaps one of curiosity. Then there are the big disruptions: the loss, the illness, the pain. We can turn towards those too, though they may be much bigger and a bit harder to wrap ourselves around. But, really, is there a difference aside from magnitude? All of these things are the disruptions of life, and these disruptions, by extension, ARE life. Turning away from them is denying what truly is right in front of us, fighting the experience that our senses scream at us is true.

Radical acceptance is acknowledging that good and bad happen, will happen, and have happened, and we can't change things that have already occurred. But we are not powerless. We have the power to control our reactions to these events. Do we manage them with grace and equanimity, informed by both emotion and wisdom? Or do we cling to what "should be" and respond solely from a place of emotional reactivity? We have the ability to move into these disruptions, to live powerfully and meaningfully within disruption, and to allow our own true selves and values to shine brightly even when we are in pain.

I could tell you stories of lives that I have witnessed transformed by disruption, and I'm sure you have similar stories from your own life and the lives of those you love. I'm sure the owners of these lives likely wish these disruptions had never been, but I have seen firsthand how they have allowed people to transform their personal pain into support, kindness, and advocacy for others. I think of the cancer survivor who becomes a champion for early detection, the parent who has lost a child who lifts up other parents in their mourning periods, and the many individuals I know whose paths in life are more difficult due to different needs, and translate this into fierce advocacy for policy changes. The acceptance of the disruption and the acknowledgment of the deep and lasting impact upon these individuals' lives allowed these transformations to happen. Like a body scarred, the wound no longer bleeds, but the silvery scar tissue stands as a reminder of both our fragility and our ever-resilient strength.

In practice this week, look for the disrupted moments. Examine them with curiosity. What are their stories? What emotions are evoked? And how are you experiencing those emotions in terms of physiological sensations and thoughts? Do you have urges for actions? How do those feelings, thoughts, sensations, and urges change as you pay attention to them and sit with them, rather than actively attempting to change or deny them? Can you use these experiences to tap into your inner needs and values, and if so, how does this inform your response?

Reflection and Implementation Tool

My main takeaways from this chapter:

My goal to use this in my own life:

Specific opportunities I may have to use this strategy or skill:

Obstacles to using this skill and meeting this goal:

Reflection and Implementation Tool

How to problem solve these obstacles

My commitment to use this skill (rate 0-10):

After implementation, here is my reflection on how this worked for me:

Raindrop moments where I can use this skill in the future:

Chapter 21: Be Scared and Do it Anyway

What: Experience bravery not by ignoring fear but by acknowledging it.

Why: Someone recently asked me to share about a time when I was brave. In our current super hero enthused culture, we have lots of ideas about bravery and courage. Often fueled by super powers that sprung from adversity (I'm looking at you, radioactive insects), the hero takes on bad guys and courts death time and time again without breaking a sweat.

How about you? For me, a radioactive insect might be enough for me to break into a sweat!

It might be easy to find examples of being brave in hindsight. We knew we had to do a thing, it was a difficult, frightening, or risky thing to do, and we did it. When we tell these stories, we might get focused on the thing, the risk, and the completion. Bravo! It's done.

But when we actually "do the thing," my guess is most of us are terrified. We feel the feeling of fear, and we "do the thing" anyway. Why?

I've already addressed our desire to push away negative emotion states. They don't feel good, and aside from the occasional cathartic rom-com generated tear fest, we don't really enjoy them. Our culture isn't super accepting of them either; stop crying, pull yourself up by your bootstraps, and "just do it."

If strong emotion states are like the sensory organs for our value system, then fear tells us something important. I'm not talking about my earlier "don't fall off the cliff" example, which reflects a true physical risk. I'm talking about the fears that leave no physical damage such as fear of stepping outside of our comfort zone, fear of failure, fear of breaking the mold. When we experience this kind of fear, we can sit with it, explore it, and perhaps recognize that it can co-exist with action. That to me is "brave;" be scared and still do the scary thing.

How: Notice those moments in your week when fear holds you back. It could be great big fear or it could be just a slight "I don't want to rock the boat" fear. Use your best mindful attention to turn towards the fear and explore what it tells you. You could do this through a formal meditation practice. Rather than pushing away, avoiding, minimizing, or rationalizing the fear, sit with it and explore it. What story is it telling you? Is that story true? Helpful? Realistic?

Sometimes fear of change, failure, and transition is fueled by untrue stories we tell ourselves. What if we can acknowledge those stories as just that--stories--and bring a clear beginner's mind to these situations, assessing their risks and rewards individually and free of preconceived notions? What would we learn about why these things frighten us? What message from our deepest soul might we hear about our unique purposes and passions if we listen long enough to explore beneath the fear?

Can you sit with fear and uncover your fuel, your courage, your bravery? And can you acknowledge the fear and, frightened, still do the thing?

Reflection and Implementation Tool

My main takeaways from this chapter:

My goal to use this in my own life:

Specific opportunities I may have to use this strategy or skill:

Obstacles to using this skill and meeting this goal:

Reflection and Implementation Tool

How to problem solve these obstacles

My commitment to use this skill (rate 0-10):

After implementation, here is my reflection on how this worked for me:

Raindrop moments where I can use this skill in the future:

Chapter 22: If You're Gonna Worry, Then Worry

What: Bring your attention fully to bear on worry so that you can manage it more productively.

Why: Can you believe it? I'm a psychologist and I'm telling you to worry. Stick with me. I'll explain.

Our mind is highly skilled at presenting us with ideas, solutions, puzzles, and questions. Sometimes this tendency leads to highly creative pursuits, fueling us with unique approaches to problems and artful and imaginative ideas. But sometimes our brain's ability to think of information from all different angles leads to worry. We can be puzzling something through and quickly get caught in a trap of "what if." And those "what if thoughts" often spiral into a series of what ifs with no recognizable solution.

When our brain tries to puzzle something through, it generally is trying to problem solve. Problem solving is great. But try problem solving in less-than-ideal conditions, such as when you are missing key pieces of information, when you're tired or hungry (or, worse, hangry), when you're highly emotionally aroused, or when you're physically ill or out of sorts. Doesn't go so well, does it? That's when we get stuck on worry, which I like to reframe as problem solving with missing parts or without the ability to step back and reasonably say "good enough."

When we're not in the frame of mind or privy to the information we need to solve a problem, it's probably in our best interest to acknowledge that and mindfully redirect our attention elsewhere. We can make a plan for problem solving in the future, when our physical needs are met, and/or when we have all the pertinent information for decision making. This practice is not seeking to totally escape problems, as that would not be realistic, fully conscious living, but to acknowledge the best circumstances for productive problem solving.

How: Your job is to notice the nature of your mind and send up a red flag when you are spiraling into a course of worry. What are your warning signs? For lots of people, it's sympathetic nervous system arousal, AKA fight or flight response. While everyone will experience this slightly differently, you might notice your heart rate increasing, your breathing growing rapid and shallow, your muscles tensing (often in the shoulders and neck), a pit in your stomach or a headache forming. Try to tune into what your body does and notice your unique constellation of warning signs.

You may notice some mental warning signs, too. How do you talk to yourself when you are problem solving, and how do you talk to yourself when you are worrying? I'm going to guess there are some key differences, and one might be the tendency to get stuck on what if thoughts when you're worrying. You'll recognize "what if" thoughts by the fact that they don't have a clear answer, and they can often be replaced by another "what if" thought. Never fully satisfied, these thoughts pull you into a spiral of worry, fear, and even panic.

Maybe you notice urges when you are worrying. We like to seek out comfort and distraction when we are caught in negative emotional states. While it probably isn't very productive to worry, it may also not be productive to replace your worry with an online shopping spree, with eating a double fudge sundae that goes against your nutritional goals, or with staying up past midnight binging on tv shows when you have an early morning.

Now that you know your emotional, behavioral, and mental warning signs for worry, choose to acknowledge them and take a different stance. "I see you, worry, I know what you are. I am having worried thoughts, my shoulders are tense, and I'm having the urge to avoid, distract, and escape." Pat yourself on the back for being mindfully aware of the worry spiral. You might also reconnect with the present moment to determine if you have something that requires worry at the moment. Are you presently safe? Are your basic needs being met? If so, then you are, physiologically, ok. Your brain's fight or flight response may be triggered but can be easily reset as you are, in fact, ok.

If you are not in the midst of an issue that needs to be immediately solved, you can decide if you want to worry right now or not. If you have the time and this is an important issue, go for it! That's right, worry! Only, don't just worry; problem solve. Gather up all the information, make a list of pros and cons, think through any missing information, and figure out how to get that information. If there is too much information missing, you may need to end your problem-solving session with a decision to revisit this issue in the future. Well done!

On the other hand, if it's not the time to worry, acknowledge that, too. "I know my brain wants to solve this problem but right now it is 3am and my focus is on sleeping," or "I'm really hungry and I will think better after lunch," or "I need to remain focused on my work project but can solve this problem when I'm done." Commend your brain on the urge to work through this problem, and remind yourself that you will do so, later. If some part of you has the bothersome thought of "I'll forget the details later!" then by all means jot them down on paper. You can keep the paper nearby and contain any thoughts or ideas as they present, but then redirect your focus to whatever your task at hand involves. Set a time for problem solving; maybe agree with yourself that you'll spend fifteen minutes working through the problem at 3pm. Great! Do it! You might find that if you are a super productive problem-solver because you give 100% of your attention to problem solving, you won't even need fifteen minutes.

But if you spend your fully allotted time and haven't solved your problem yet, it may be that you have missing information or it is not a problem that you alone can solve. That's ok, and maybe mindfully acknowledging this will help your brain to move on. You can return to the problem when there is new information available to help you problem-solve.

Reflection and Implementation Tool

My main takeaways from this chapter:

My goal to use this in my own life:

Specific opportunities I may have to use this strategy or skill:

Obstacles to using this skill and meeting this goal:

Reflection and Implementation Tool

How to problem solve these obstacles

....

....

....

My commitment to use this skill (rate 0-10):

....

....

....

After implementation, here is my reflection on how this worked for me:

....

....

....

Raindrop moments where I can use this skill in the future:

....

....

....

Chapter 23: Life-Sized Emotions

What: Keep your emotions life-sized--not too big, not too small, just right--so you can respond to them appropriately.

Why: I was driving to work recently on a highway that was under construction. The workers were in the process of mounting new overhead signs. You've probably seen the signs I'm talking about hundreds of times: green, rectangular exit and direction signs that list the upcoming exits and how many miles to each. The signs were on the pavement at eye level as I drove by. Those signs are HUGE. I was floored by the size of them, since normally when we drive under them, they are a good 20 or more feet up in the air, and we are viewing them on our approach from 100 or so feet away. We almost never see them at life size, and, hence, their "reduced viewing size" becomes our impression of their true size.

The experience led me to thinking about our emotions. The opposite happens with our emotions--whereas the highway sign is huge but appears "normal," emotions that are "normal" can appear to be huge, especially when we compare them to our rational thought processes. Why exactly does this happen?

It all goes back to fight or flight response. Negative emotions--fear and anger in particular--signal there is danger in our world. These emotions occur when information from our senses triggers our sympathetic nervous system to activate. This sends energy to our muscles, speeds up our heart rate and breathing, and prepares us to ward off an aggressor or run for safety: the fight or flight response. So those emotions are protective.

A big discharge of emotions, from an evolutionary standpoint, is a surefire way to keep us safe. And those early humans who had big emotional responses were more likely to stay safe. Through the process of evolution, those individuals were more likely to survive and pass along their genetic information (including big emotional responses) to their offspring. Over the millennia, our DNA veered towards the side of emotional overreaction, especially with regards to the negative. If you find food, you'll survive another few days. But if you become food, you'll never eat (or do anything else) again.

Most of us, I hope, are not daily trying to fight off aggressors or run to safety. But our nervous systems are still designed for an unsafe world. When negative emotions hit, they are big, larger than life, so that we will respond in kind and stay safe, even if what we are threatened by is a minor, non-lethal, garden-variety frustration. Take back your sanity by bringing those emotions back down to life size!

How: First, notice your warning signs. We all experience the mental, behavioral, and physiological signs of large emotions in slightly different ways, though most of these sequelae can be traced back to some level of fight or flight response. Maybe your warning sign is sweating, heart racing, or muscle tension. Maybe you are more apt to notice yourself spinning into "what if" thoughts or "this always happens to me, life is so unfair" thoughts. Or maybe, behaviorally, you have an urge to run, to avoid, or to use a strategy that will rapidly change your emotions.

Get really clear on your warning signs, perhaps by meditating formally on recent events that have led to large emotional responses. Rather than trying to change those emotions, sit with them and explore them without judgment. Perhaps try moving into an attitude of compassion towards that primitive, safety-seeking part of the brain that just wants to keep us well.

Once you're better aware of your warning signs, you can use these as your signal that you're entering "big emotion" territory. When you make this connection, give yourself a pat on the back for being mindful. Now you can decide; do you want to respond to these emotions or react to these emotions?

When we react to emotions, on some level our brain decides they are correct and worth listening to. We have a burst of anger, and we follow where anger leads us. We pop off at someone or type out an angry email tirade. We assume that our enormous emotions are actually true to life and worthy of a huge reaction, and then feel vindicated in whatever firestorm we unleash around us.

When we respond to emotions, we turn mindful awareness to the experience and then allow wisdom to guide our decisions. We notice the anger and explore the anger, then decide if blasting someone verbally or through an email is in our best interests and would be a helpful way to solve whatever led to the anger. Using mindful awareness, we can bring our emotions back down to a realistic size and allow wisdom to determine our response.

Reflection and Implementation Tool

My main takeaways from this chapter:

My goal to use this in my own life:

Specific opportunities I may have to use this strategy or skill:

Obstacles to using this skill and meeting this goal:

Reflection and Implementation Tool

How to problem solve these obstacles

My commitment to use this skill (rate 0-10):

After implementation, here is my reflection on how this worked for me:

Raindrop moments where I can use this skill in the future:

Chapter 24: Open to Vulnerable Possibility

What: Are you buttoned up in the armor of self-protection, or do you allow yourself to turn towards vulnerable possibility?

Why: Life pushes us. While there are plenty of moments of celebration, there are also times when we circle the wagons, hunker down, and endure. Grief, loss, fear, abandonment, embarrassment... we can probably all dig into the vaults of discomfort and find ample examples of such times.

As we've explored previously, our nervous system is finely tuned to protect the species, which works fabulously if we are in an unsafe environment. And our environment can certainly feel very unsafe at times. But the kind of safety that our nervous system provides is physical safety from life-or-death scenarios. And while we may have some of these experiences in our lives, hopefully they are infrequent and not recurring.

The psychic sense of being unsafe is different. It is our judging mind running amok. The situations that create these unpleasant emotions are very real, and the emotional reactions are real: a death, a loss of a job, a worry about finances, the end of a relationship. But it is the judging mind that pushes these from upsetting but manageable parts of the human condition, to a nervous system interpretation of a life-or-death scenario. That's not good for us. Physically, it creates a stressed and hyperactivated sympathetic nervous system, and unleashes high levels of cortisol which have an aging effect on the body.

When we can balance out the judging mind with an attitude of hopeful expectation, we can turn towards vulnerable possibility. We can allow room for the chance that something good may happen, and take the vulnerable step towards change-creating actions. Without being vulnerable, we remain static and stuck. Safe, but not safe in the space our souls truly long to blossom.

If you have ever taken a risk to push yourself towards an idea such as a relationship you are trying to deepen or grow, a job opportunity, a creative pursuit, you've probably moved into this space of discomfort and vulnerability, and perhaps have your own stories of the possibilities that blossomed. The book you are holding in your hand is one such example for myself. Writing this book was a risk. Will it sell? Will people like it? Will it be useful? In many ways, I could not write and stay safe from potential criticism, failure, and rejection. But I know that I would not be happy contained in such a space where I cannot share my ideas, so I temper the risk of failure with the hopeful expectation that these words resonate with some of my readers.

How: This "how" is less of a specific how, but more of a mindset shift to approach. You might start with some meditative reflection on moments of possibility, where you are poised on the step between safe and vulnerable. Perhaps an action that feels risky or a situation in which you might fail could also be a situation that provides the possibility for success and achievement. Often, this is accompanied by a feeling of uncertainty; you could succeed, or you could have what feels like a failure.

Notice how our brain loves to jump in and judge this. A failure could just be a different sort of opportunity, the chance to gather information that will inform our future behavior. But our nervous system's desire to keep us safe locks in on the possibility of danger.

When you notice such a situation in your own life, sit with the emotions that arise. Acknowledge and feel them. Allow them to show up and share their stories, and then listen for other stories. Can you be open to fear and hope at the same time? Can they both be given the grace to exist within you, while wisdom allows you to turn vulnerably towards what might be possible?

In your day-to-day life, you might use these strong emotions as a barometer, letting you know that you are on the brink of something new. However, you sense this uniquely in your body, perhaps as discomfort, rapid heart rate, thoughts of fear or thoughts of failure. Use those indicators to alert you that you've arrived at an opportunity to be vulnerable. Just notice this and sit with it. Acknowledge the feelings, and notice the tendency to engage in your internal narrative about the feelings. And then, gently, try to notice any possibility and opportunity. Can you feel vulnerability? Can you entertain thoughts of a positive outcome by taking a risk?

When we open to these possibilities, we can begin to take gentle risks in ways that serve us. We will likely have some successes, and some failures. We are guaranteed safety when we take no risks, but we are also stripped of the opportunity for success and growth. Gaining confidence through gentle risks and positive outcomes, we are likely to find more strength and openness to vulnerability in the future.

Reflection and Implementation Tool

My main takeaways from this chapter:

My goal to use this in my own life:

Specific opportunities I may have to use this strategy or skill:

Obstacles to using this skill and meeting this goal:

Reflection and Implementation Tool

How to problem solve these obstacles

_____

_____

_____

My commitment to use this skill (rate 0-10):

_____

_____

_____

After implementation, here is my reflection on how this worked for me:

_____

_____

_____

Raindrop moments where I can use this skill in the future:

_____

_____

_____

Chapter 25: Let it Pass

What: Sit with uncomfortable emotions with curiosity.

Why: Emotions are temporary. They are a part of our bodies' safety mechanisms. This is especially true for uncomfortable emotions such as anxiety, fear, embarrassment, guilt, and anger. Strong negative emotions are often the early detection system of safety issues in our environment, which could include threats to personal safety or threats to relational safety. By relational safety, I'm referring to events or actions that could cause harm in relationships. This may not seem like a "true" safety issue to us in the 21st century, but for evolving humans (when our DNA was laid down and solidified), upsetting the group could lead to social ostracization, which would be a true safety issue when you are relying on others for wellbeing.

When we have a strong uncomfortable emotion, therefore, we are hardwired to get rid of it. Typically, this moves us into some kind of action to eliminate the emotion. For fear and anxiety, we often choose actions that serve as avoidance strategies. Rationally, that makes a lot of sense. If you are fearful of your boss' reaction to a project you worked on, you might avoid setting a meeting to review the project. While that may temporarily decrease the fear, in the long-term it builds the anticipatory fear. That meeting will happen eventually and may create new problems; now you are fearful your boss will be angry that you delayed completion of the project. Anger is a highly activating, energizing emotion. It fuels quick responses, which is great if you are in a life-or-death situation. It is not so great if you are managing a sensitive issue or working to maintain relationships. Anger can be a true catalyst for change but when discharged without wisdom, it could leave a trail of scorched relationships in its wake.

The emotional centers of our brain are closely connected to the sensory relay station of the brain, the thalamus. As the thalamus relays information about safety to our limbic system, where emotional reaction and fight-or-flight responses originate, it also relays that information to the thinking part of the brain, the cerebral cortex. But those strong emotional reactions to incoming information (and sometimes to our own thoughts) often occur before we have consciously processed the information and determined a mindful, wisdom-informed response; in other words, we feel before we think. We can bring mindful awareness to our emotional reactions to let the ones that don't serve us pass and to glean helpful information about our values.

How: This week, be on the lookout for really strong emotional reactions. I've talked mostly about negative reactions, but be aware of positive reactions as well. As these opportunities present, take a moment or two to sit with them in mindful awareness.

Close your eyes if it is an appropriate time to do so. Notice how you are experiencing the emotion in your body. Emotions at their most primitive are a combination of physical sensation and mental interpretation. Notice where in your body you feel the emotion, and notice every aspect of that sensation. Is it warm, cold, sharp, dull, pulsing, steady, shifting? Does the feeling move throughout your body and change with time? What happens to the feeling when you focus on it?

Also notice the thoughts that arise that are connected to the emotion. When you step back and watch your thoughts mindfully, do you notice themes that come up? Can you be a curious observer of your thoughts, perhaps noting "that's interesting, tell me more" as each thought presents? Are your thoughts suggesting that the situation leading to your strong reaction has triggered a habitual reaction from prior situations? If so, is your current situation worthy of the same response or is it unique and in need of its own specific response?

As you sit with your thoughts and feelings without an immediate response, you may uncover dissonance in your value system. Understanding this dissonance and choosing an action that is respectful of your value system will likely release the strong emotion and allow you to move forward on a path that is authentic and helpful to you. For instance, if a co-worker or family member asks you to complete a task and you notice a flash of anger and habitual thoughts of "why do I always have to do the dirty work," this could signal a true pattern in your relationship, or it could signal an assumption on your part (that the other person is not doing any of "the dirty work" and foisting it all on you). Reacting negatively toward this person in anger may relieve you of the immediate task at hand, but may create other problems (a reputation in the office as a "hot head," for example) and will not clarify your assumption that undesired work is being dumped on you.

If you had this experience and sat with it for a few moments before reacting, you might identify the underlying issue: feeling disrespected and put-upon by a team member. Moving through the uncomfortable emotion to a space of wisdom might allow you to take a different action, such as returning to the other team member to ask for clarification, to share your perspective of being asked to "do the dirty work," and seeking the other person's perspective. Perhaps they think you are a really good deliverer of difficult news and seek your support, not out of a space of burdening you but out of valuing your ability to have such conversations. Maybe they are unaware of the pattern of behavior in which they ask you to do these difficult things on a regular basis. We could probably come up with a lot of different potential outcomes to this scenario. Ultimately, though, without clarification and discussion, the pattern will continue. This space of wisdom brought by curiously observing the emotion and letting it pass allows you to connect deeper with values and plan a course of values informed action.

Reflection and Implementation Tool

My main takeaways from this chapter:

My goal to use this in my own life:

Specific opportunities I may have to use this strategy or skill:

Obstacles to using this skill and meeting this goal:

Reflection and Implementation Tool

How to problem solve these obstacles

....

....

....

My commitment to use this skill (rate 0-10):

....

....

After implementation, here is my reflection on how this worked for me:

....

....

....

Raindrop moments where I can use this skill in the future:

....

....

....

Section 3: Mindfulness, Values, and Intentionality

Chapter 26: Identifying Intentions

What: Set goals using a mindful examination of your values for action that resonates with your soul.

Why: There are several times throughout the year that call upon us to set goals and resolutions. It could be the first of the calendar year, the beginning of a school year, the beginning of a fiscal or tax-season year, the birth of a child, or the start of a new job. Whether your "new year" follows a calendar event or comes about as a transitional point in your life, these moments fill us with a desire for change and motivation to take on new habits.

And then, like clockwork, those goals and resolutions are cast aside. Our zeal for change quickly evaporates, and we are left with the reality of the dedication and hard work needed for change to occur and for habits to be formed. The fitness center that is bursting in January is a ghost town in April. We still want that rockin' beach bod the magazines convinced us to go for, but the early morning sweat sessions robbing us of shut-eye just aren't super appealing long-term. Why do we fail?

To be successful, goals should start with an examination of our values within an area of life. What do we feel most passionate about, and how does that passion inform a specific life domain, such as family relationships, self-care, finance, or any other life-domain? Starting from our values, we can identify intentions and goals that align with our truest selves. The values provide motivation to reach goals that will last beyond the new year's excitement. For example, a goal to "get in shape" is a common new year's resolution. If a person adopts this goal solely because they think they should and they see other people holding this goal, they have little personal motivation to achieve (other than, perhaps, to be viewed in a positive light by peers). If a person connects deeply to values that inform this goal, for instance, values of health, longevity, and wellness, they are more likely to connect with the actions that lead to the goal.

How: Figuring out what you value may take a lot of introspection. There are a variety of exercises that might help you connect with your values. Imagine you are writing your obituary, or looking back from the end of your life on a scrapbook of your life. What do you want to see there? How would you like to be described? At the end of it all, when all the little stuff is swept away, what big stuff is left? You might meditate on this, or journal, and see what presents itself to you. Try not to become overly caught up in where you've already been. This is about looking forward and planning what you would like for the rest of your life.

Another practice is to list your musts, your priorities in life. Again, don't sweat the small stuff here but figure out your non-negotiables. Don't worry about how that has played out for you in the past. This is about dreaming forward to what is most important to your future self. What are the absolutes that you would like to be able to reflect on at the end of your life?

When you have connected with your deepest values through reflection, journaling, meditation, spiritual practices, or however they present best to you, you can then be clear on your reasons for change. You might find it helpful to write down your why, perhaps by crafting a mission statement. It might start off big and general—I want to live a life of authenticity, I want to be remembered as a compassionate person, I want to prioritize my physical, emotional, and spiritual health. Once you better understand your values, you can work to be intentional about how they play out in your life.

Clear intentions allow you to craft specific, measurable, and time sensitive goals. I'll share more on the science of goal setting in the next chapter.

Reflection and Implementation Tool

My main takeaways from this chapter:

My goal to use this in my own life:

Specific opportunities I may have to use this strategy or skill:

Obstacles to using this skill and meeting this goal:

Reflection and Implementation Tool

How to problem solve these obstacles

My commitment to use this skill (rate 0-10):

After implementation, here is my reflection on how this worked for me:

Raindrop moments where I can use this skill in the future:

Chapter 27: Mindful Goal Setting

What: Set a goal, make it achievable, and turn it into habit.

Why: We love to set goals. Aspiring to be better, faster, smarter, more productive, leaner, stronger, healthier...the list goes on. Set with optimism and hope for change, the creation of goals is an attempt to align our behavior with our value system. Want more family in your life? Then set a goal to improve family connections. Want financial security? Then set a goal to increase finances. Like the idea of a healthier future? Then set a goal to improve your health.

To bridge from values to goal attainment, we need to state our goals in terms of achievable, measurable behaviors. Psychologists call these "operationalized" goals. They are observable and we can mark progress towards the goal. You may have heard these referred to as SMART goals (specific, measurable, achievable, relevant, and time-bound).

We'll bring mindful awareness to the process of goal setting and attainment, with a nod to problem solving the obstacles along the way.

How: The first step is to identify your goal. To stick with the example I've used above, we'll explore a goal of "improve family connections," related to the value of positive family relationships. Before digging into the definition of a goal, you might bring mindful awareness to the why of your goal. In my example, a reasonable "why" would be valuing family. With your own goal, bring awareness to how you chose the goal, why it resonates with you, and any other motivations for achieving the goal. This will help you stay the course even if the road to your goal is bumpy. Using the SMART goal acronym, the "why" for the goal addresses its relevance.

The second step is to restate your goal to make it specific, measurable, achievable, and time-bound. You may have to set multiple objectives for a specific goal. In my example of improving family connections, we might have overarching objectives of increasing pleasantness of family interactions from a rating of 5 out of 10 to a rating of 7 out of 10. Or, in plain English, from "meh" to "pretty good." That's measurable (albeit subjective), and it's probably achievable. If I had said to make it a 10 out of 10 at all times, that would likely not be achievable. However, it's not particularly specific or time-bound.

I can further break down that goal of increasing pleasantness of family interactions into specific, time-bound actions. I might notice that to have more pleasant interactions, the family needs to spend more time together on joint tasks. I might therefore plan to have a weekly family game night, a bi-monthly "special dinner" chosen and prepared by the family together, and a compliments jar where family members can write compliments about each other to be read aloud during the special dinner. These discrete actions help us move from a fairly nebulous but valuable goal to specific steps in which we can engage.

We can also apply the SMART goal strategy to work situations. A frequent work goal people have is to promote within their organization. I always start with the relevance or values behind the goal. In this situation, the values could be related to finances, to what these finances mean for an individual's family (for instance, supporting the value of education by saving for college), and it could reflect values related to achievement, contribution, and purpose. These are just a few examples as there are a lot of ways that a person's career could tick off values boxes. Making a promotion specific, measurable, achievable, and time-bound, might involve key performance indicators related to promoting (specific and measurable actions), make sure we have the skill set to perform these actions or seeking out these skills (making the goal achievable), and setting a timeline for completion of these actions.

While working on goals, we can bring mindful attention to the process of achieving the goal. What do we notice in our thoughts, our emotions, and in our bodily sensations as we engage in these steps? What is smooth, and what is more challenging? Is our judging mind getting in our way? Can we be curious about the process instead?

A final important step in goal setting and attainment is noticing obstacles that arise while working toward the goal, and problem solving these difficulties. Mindful awareness can really help you when problem solving. By bringing awareness to moments of frustration due to obstacles, we can engage with those obstacles in a different way. Rather than avoiding the difficulty or categorizing the goal as a failure and quitting, we can turn towards the problem and explore it with curiosity. Are we facing a problem of motivation? Of poorly communicated strategy? Of a non-specific goal? Of an unreasonable timeline? All of these issues can be solved with a little creativity and nonjudgmental awareness.

Reflection and Implementation Tool

My main takeaways from this chapter:

....

....

My goal to use this in my own life:

....

....

....

Specific opportunities I may have to use this strategy or skill:

....

....

....

Obstacles to using this skill and meeting this goal:

....

....

....

Reflection and Implementation Tool

How to problem solve these obstacles

My commitment to use this skill (rate 0-10):

After implementation, here is my reflection on how this worked for me:

Raindrop moments where I can use this skill in the future:

Chapter 28: Choose It

What: Bring mindful awareness to how you narrate the stressors and tasks in your life and change your self-talk to reflect your intentions.

Why: "I have to get up early tomorrow."

"This report has to be finished by noon and I'm so over it."

"I just want to hang out and veg but I have to go exercise."

Ever say those kinds of things to yourself? You're in good company. The way we choose to narrate our existence is a powerful force. Notice that I said "choose." The way we talk to ourselves is a choice, albeit a choice to which you may not bring much attention and intention. Just like most things in life, we can use mindful attention to examine this powerful self-talk, internal narrator, and sometimes-critic.

By increasing conscious awareness of our internal dialogue, choices open up to us. Try this: tell yourself "I have to go to a social event tonight." Now try "I'm choosing to go to a social event tonight." Or even, "I get to go to a social event tonight." Subtle changes, but different emotions arise based on these statements. If you love social events and the "have to" part doesn't matter, substitute a less favored activity... work, housecleaning, grocery shopping, exercise... you get the idea.

When we consciously set intentions, we can then choose our behaviors to be congruent with our values. For instance, if we set an intention to be healthier in the new year, one logical behavioral choice would be to exercise more. We might operationalize that goal as going to the gym three times a week for 45 minutes each time. We then can remind ourselves that we are choosing this activity because it helps us move towards a specific, aligned goal.

But when we say to ourselves "I have to go to the gym today," we undermine the positive intention and negate the fact that this is a goal that we ourselves set. It's not being thrust upon us by some external force. It is the deepest desires of our being, set into behavior by careful self-examination and introspection.

If you're an adult, likely no one is forcing you to go to the gym, go to work, visit with people whose company you don't enjoy, exercise, or clean your house. When we choose to go to the gym, we are aligning our behavior with an intention to exercise in order to serve a value of wellness. When we choose to go to work, we are aligning our behavior with an intention to earn money in order to serve a value of standard of living. Clearly, there are lots of other intentions and values related to work; money is just one of the most basic and universal values met by paid jobs. When we choose to spend the day with our partner's friends whom we don't enjoy, we may be aligning our behavior with support for our partner in order to serve a value of relationship harmony.

How: Use your best mindful awareness to highlight your thought patterns and let the alarm bells ring when you catch an "I have to" thought. When you catch that thought, sit with it for a moment. Try to understand the emotions, thoughts, and urges that arise. These are worthy of attention. Next, check in with your values and intentions around the behavior in question. Are these truly your values and intentions? Did you select them based on what is best for you? If so, great. If not, you may need to do a little deeper digging. Maybe there is a relationship that needs some repair, or a work task that is no longer serving your needs and can be reassigned if possible. It could be that you'd benefit from cultivating a different assessment of the task--in what way does the less desirable task fill some value for you?

For example, once I had a job that wasn't well-aligned with my professional goals. In hindsight, it was a fabulous opportunity and growth experience for me, but at the time I couldn't see into the future to fully appreciate this. But it was a very family friendly place to work, and when I had my first child, I was allowed a good deal of flexibility in setting my schedule. When I used the metric of professional goals to determine my satisfaction and my "why" for the job, I was in an "I have to go to work" mindset. When I re-evaluated the situation and decided that, at that point in my life, the most important aspects of my job were that it allowed me flexibility and adequate finances to grow my family, I felt much more satisfied with my choice, and I could "choose" to go to work.

As you explore this, identify any sticky points in the process, work to understand them, and then flip the script to reflect how these initially dreaded activities may be serving you. It's kind of like looking for the silver lining. And I'm not just being Pollyanna here. Something attracted you to the activity in the first place. Bring your mindful attention to these values and allow them to clarify your behavior. Then inform your internal narrator to change the script to reflect your true intentions.

Reflection and Implementation Tool

My main takeaways from this chapter:

My goal to use this in my own life:

Specific opportunities I may have to use this strategy or skill:

Obstacles to using this skill and meeting this goal:

Reflection and Implementation Tool

How to problem solve these obstacles

My commitment to use this skill (rate 0-10):

After implementation, here is my reflection on how this worked for me:

Raindrop moments where I can use this skill in the future:

Chapter 29: Intentional To-Do Lists

What: Use your to-do list as an opportunity for intentional focus and a tool for goal attainment.

Why: To-do lists are probably everyone's go-to option for planning and prioritization. But have you stopped and given thought to how you use a to-do list and how it serves you? Some people experience great stress at the thought of having a to-do list, or in its more formal incarnation, a planner. It might feel like a set up for failure, a pressure filled list of expectations, or even another job to create the plan.

Personally, I've been guilty of making "mindless" to-do lists; lists loaded with way more than I can possibly accomplish. While they may include all the things I'd like to do, they are not all things that are practical to do in a relatively short (day or two) period of time. My husband has found these lists and, interpreting them incorrectly as a "honey do" list or list of things I want HIM to do, has humorously dubbed them ("correctly" dubbed them, he opines upon editing this chapter) my "secret lists."

While there's no harm in writing out long-term goals and plans--and in fact, I'd encourage it--putting big goals on a daily to-do list may not be your best option. Let's take a look at goal setting and time management to get super mindful about what makes a daily to-do list that serves you well.

How: You might want to start the to-do list exercise with a brain dump. Start writing down all the items that come to mind for today. Don't edit yourself, just let the plans flow. We'll work on prioritization and pragmatic considerations next.

You have some options as to how you approach this exercise. You could go with paper, pen, and a traditional list format. You might like to put each item on a small sticky note and spread the notes out on your desk. Finally, you could manage this list digitally--use one of the many list applications, use a word processing or spreadsheet page, or use a project planning system like Trello, Asana, ClickUp, Airtable, or a myriad other tools (just search for "project planners").

Regardless of what system you choose, start by dumping your daily items. Once you have done this, you can start a mindful sort of these items. Consider each item and next to it (perhaps in different colors of pen) record any hard deadlines. Next, consider each item and think about how much time each task will take. You will likely have some fast tasks (calls to make, emails to return, things to schedule) as well as tasks that will take considerably longer. Sort your tasks into those that will take under an hour and those that will take over an hour.

Return to the tasks that will take over an hour and consider if you can break any of these tasks down into components. For instance, if "write this manuscript" were on my list, not only would that be an overwhelming daily to-do item, I probably wouldn't have a great idea of where to start. I might have an end goal of producing this book, but I need some actionable steps that I can make progress on in order to generate a feeling of accomplishment and sustain my motivation to eventually finish the task. I could break down "write this manuscript" into research need for books on mindfulness (perhaps a 30-minute task), construct a framework for how I want to approach my writing (30 minutes), create a very rough outline (30 minutes), and begin brainstorming ideas for individual chapters (30 minutes). That would be a solid two hours of work towards a task that, in reality, will take me many months of consistent daily work to complete. And knowing my own limits for writing, I'm not going to stack a day with eight hours of writing time. I will burn out, my creativity will run dry, and what I produce will feel forced and lack inspiration. Similarly, where you have large goals, consider the first several steps and a reasonable amount of time you can spend on them today.

Now that you have estimated time lines and actionable items for longer term goals, start looking at deadlines. I'm going to suggest you apply the Eisenhower Matrix to your items. On paper, you can draw a simple x-y matrix (a large cross dividing your paper into 4 squares). In a project planning program, you could make each square a list. Label your quadrants, moving from upper left quadrant clockwise to lower left quadrant (1) Urgent and Important, (2) Urgent and Not Important, (3) Not Urgent and

Not Important, and (4) Not Urgent and Important. Start moving your items to these quadrants, or number them if you're working on a sheet of paper.

Urgent and Important items get top priority. They may be items that have reached crisis level in terms of timing and require us to act now. Fortunately, these are often very discrete items that can be ticked off your list quickly. Important and Not Urgent items are typically our own goals, long-term plans, and proactive work on projects. Working on items in this quadrant results in fewer fires to put out, as we complete them with energy and motivation before they move into the Important and Urgent column and require swift attention.

Urgent and Not Important items might be important to someone else, or they might be distractions. Phone calls, responding to email, interruptions, piles of correspondence on our desk; they all have the illusion of true urgency but they pull us out of the quality time spent on non-urgent but important tasks. Look at your Urgent/Not Important items, set time frames for them, and try to contain them within those time frames. Perhaps you set aside 20 minutes first thing in the morning, at lunch, and at the end of the day to respond to email, phone calls, text messages, or whatever other urgent but not important items pull you away from your true work. Urgent and Not Important items are also great items to delegate if you have that luxury. Give them to an assistant, set up an email auto responder with your "office hours" for returning calls and a link to a webpage that answers frequently asked questions, or work to minimize these items by moving them to people for whom they are important. For example, if your teen child needs to sign up for a field trip, they are likely able to navigate the payment portal and complete all permission slip information on their own, then bring it to you to sign.

Last, you'll have items that are Not Urgent and Not Important. Know what to do with them? If they bring you joy, then make them important and schedule time for them. If they truly do not enhance your life, let them go without guilt. If they are important to someone who is important to you, if possible, delegate them to that person and ask them to enlist your help as needed.

Once you've sorted your to-do list mindfully, with a nod to pragmatic time considerations and relative importance, you'll be on your way to intentional accomplishment rather than getting bogged down on time wasters. You can also treat this list building exercise as an opportunity to bring awareness while adding items to your list. Perhaps you pay attention to items that trigger feelings of tension or discomfort, and determine what this is about prior to adding an item to a list. Items that frequently appear on the list but are not accomplished also beg some deliberate consideration. Are these items reflective of your values, or are they "shoulds" that you've borrowed from others, or are they tasks foisted on you without your investment?

Reflection and Implementation Tool

My main takeaways from this chapter:

My goal to use this in my own life:

Specific opportunities I may have to use this strategy or skill:

Obstacles to using this skill and meeting this goal:

Reflection and Implementation Tool

How to problem solve these obstacles

My commitment to use this skill (rate 0-10):

After implementation, here is my reflection on how this worked for me:

Raindrop moments where I can use this skill in the future:

Chapter 30: Wherever You Are, Be There Fully

What: Embrace your current moment with 100% of your being by focusing on the now and not on outcomes and goals.

Why: Thich Nhat Hanh, a Vietnamese Buddhist monk and mindfulness scholar, writes, "We don't cook in order to have food to eat. We don't wash dishes to have clean dishes. We cook to cook, and we wash dishes to wash dishes. The purpose is not to get these chores out of the way in order to do something more meaningful."

The mind is a pretty powerful place, especially when we find ourselves dwelling there. I can't fully back this up, but I'd argue that we are probably the only species that spends so much time dwelling in the mind. Also arguably, why we have had success as a species, and have figured out how to navigate not only our native planet but the stars. While there is clearly a time and a place for dwelling in the mind (dreaming, planning, problem-solving, anticipating, and directing), there's also a strong argument to spend at least some of our time being fully present to our current reality.

So, when you wash dishes, do you wash dishes, or do you strive for clean dishes? It's a pretty subtle distinction. Let me tell you how that sorts out for me.

Me, "striving for clean dishes": "Hmmm there is a whole sink full of dishes. I live with four other people. Why am I cleaning the dishes? This is gross! Someone should have rinsed these first. Uh oh, we need to buy more detergent as it's running low. I wonder what else we need at the store? (exits into mental review of the kitchen inventory, meal plans for the next 5 nights of dinner)."

Me, "washing dishes": noticing the water feels warm. Noticing the slippery feel of the soap. Noticing the weight of the dish in my hands. Noticing the lemon smell of the soap. Noticing the lightness of the near empty soap bottle. Noticing the pressure as I scrub at a dish and the tightness in the muscles of my forearm, noticing some enjoyment at the appearance of a clean dish.

See the difference? So easily do we enter into the judging and planning mind, that we lose the current moment which presents us with ample opportunities to practice mindful attention. I've had people ask if shutting off this internal chatter is actually just "distraction" from what we need to do. The reality is, if I was fully present while washing my dishes, I still noticed that the soap was nearly empty. But I recognized that it was not the time to make a shopping list and redirected my attention to the task at hand. I might have also noticed some judgments about other people not doing the dishes, but I consciously chose not to make that my focus. Had I done so, a relatively neutral or even pleasant task would turn into drudgery. If needing more help with dishes is truly a message my soul needs me to hear and to communicate to others, I can do that, but probably not while I'm washing dishes.

How: You can use almost any regular task to bring 100% of your attention and focus to the present moment. Routine chores and events provide a perfect practice opportunity for in-the-moment mindful awareness, because you probably can do them without thinking too hard. Dishes, cleaning tasks, taking a shower, driving a well-known route in the car, and exercising are just a few ideas for daily activities that provide a rich source of present moment experiences.

When you select your activity, be aware of the nature of the mind to wander, narrate, and judge. Often these are urges, which you might label, such as "urge to complain about housework." Then release the urge and redirect your attention to the task. Or, if you notice your mind getting into its habit of narrating and planning, label this as "thinking about the future," and return to your task. The immediate sensory experience, what you see, hear, smell, taste, and feel, is a great way to come back 100% to the present moment.

If lots of thoughts come up, don't judge yourself. Your brain is highly skilled at thinking. That's a good thing! Commend your brain for doing its job, remind it that you're ok right now, and gently redirect your focus to what's in front of you. If you have "sticky thoughts," thoughts that seem to keep coming up despite your attempt to return to the moment, just realize that these might be important thoughts to you. Acknowledge them, and let your brain know that you'll return to them later. But right now, you have chosen to focus on the activity you're engaged in.

It takes practice, but with time you may find a routine of these brief moments of conscious, thoughtfully aware mindfulness punctuated throughout your day; in other words, true raindrop moments. Think of them as opportunities to be fully present to your world and open to the experiences that present themselves.

Reflection and Implementation Tool

My main takeaways from this chapter:

....

....

....

My goal to use this in my own life:

....

....

....

Specific opportunities I may have to use this strategy or skill:

....

....

....

Obstacles to using this skill and meeting this goal:

....

....

....

Reflection and Implementation Tool

How to problem solve these obstacles

My commitment to use this skill (rate 0-10):

After implementation, here is my reflection on how this worked for me:

Raindrop moments where I can use this skill in the future:

Chapter 31: Mindful of Money

What: Bring mindful awareness to your spending habits, so that your spending becomes intentional and values driven.

Why: You work hard for the money. You're aware of the effort that it takes to collect your paycheck. You likely lobby for pay raises and appreciate receiving them. You dedicated countless hours to your education and career, probably working your way up the ladder, perhaps taking less attractive positions earlier in your career because you knew they would build the path to your future job. You did all of that with great intentionality. Those decisions were given thought and deliberation, and you weighed the value of each job, in terms of straight up cash as well as experience, before taking it. Do you give that same intentionality to your money when it leaves your pocket?

It's gotten easier and easier to part with that hard earned dough. Tap and pay options speed you through the checkout line with barely a thought to the actual financial transaction. Webpages store your credit card online for ease of spending, and "one swipe" buying options all but eliminate the thinking behind the purchase.

The outcome isn't all roses. While retailers are probably loving it, household debt in the United States is at an all-time high, with mortgage, student loan, auto loan, and credit card debt all increasing. Total household debt has risen for the last several years. At the end of quarter 3, 2020, total household debt hit its highest ever mark at $14.35 trillion. (That's $14,350,000,000,000, in case you're wondering. It's hard for me to conceptualize such a large number.)

Yes, sometimes purchases made with credit are important. Our housing economy is such that it would be hard for most families to purchase homes without a mortgage, and, arguably, home ownership is a good investment. But much of our credit card debt is discretionary, and when it's super easy to swipe and sip a $5 latte, we can quickly get in trouble. Bringing intentionality to our spending is one way to combat this.

How: There are many ways to be more aware of how you spend, and move from mindless spending into mindfully-aware spending. Essentially, anything that breaks the tendency to spend without mindfulness will break mindless purchasing habits. Budgeting is a mindful money practice, and using cash instead of plastic can keep you true to your budget. For instance, if you budget $150 a month for snacks, coffee, and lunches during the work day, you could withdraw that money at the beginning of the month in cash, keep it in a special section of your purse or wallet, and when it's gone, it's gone. Get down to your last fiver and you'll likely pause a bit before spending it (and maybe that break room coffee will start tasting just a little bit better).

Designating credit cards for intentional purchases only is another way to be mindful about spending. Make them hard to access—put them in a lock box at home, and delete the "saved" cards from the online stores where you frequently shop. If finding your credit card and typing it in is enough to deter you from buying something online, chances are pretty high that you don't really want or need the item. Or give yourself a self-imposed time-buffer before any spending over a given amount—perhaps for any purchases over $100 other than bills or groceries, you decide to wait at least 48 hours before making the purchase. If it's a purchase that is in-line with your values, you'll buy it then. If it isn't aligned with your values, you'll have a set amount of time to reflect on the purchase in advance and be relieved that you don't buy it impulsively.

You can also tune into the sensations related to the urge to purchase and the gratification that comes from making a purchase. These dopamine hits to the brain are real.

However, we have other options for increasing our sense of gratification. Perhaps noticing the urge to purchase can trigger mindful awareness of the body's needs and reflection on how to best meet those needs before swiping the credit card.

Reflection and Implementation Tool

My main takeaways from this chapter:

My goal to use this in my own life:

Specific opportunities I may have to use this strategy or skill:

Obstacles to using this skill and meeting this goal:

Reflection and Implementation Tool

How to problem solve these obstacles

My commitment to use this skill (rate 0-10):

After implementation, here is my reflection on how this worked for me:

Raindrop moments where I can use this skill in the future:

Chapter 32: "I'm So Busy!"

What: Increase awareness and intentional use of time, and communicate that appropriately.

Why: Busy much? If you're enthusiastically nodding your head, you're not alone. Americans work, on average, more hours than people in most other industrialized nations. That comes with a downside; we have less time for other necessities and leisure. If you work in a company that has cut back on staff, you may be finding yourself doing more than one job's worth of work, also contributing to the sense of busyness. If asked, "hey, how are you?" and your gut response is, "I'm so busy," it might be worth taking a look at what you are communicating to others (and to yourself) and working to be intentional about what you are expressing.

Telling others you are "too busy" comes with a cost. It can be interpreted as bragging (a no-no in most social structures). It can communicate that you are not available, which can cut you off for advancement or other growth opportunities, and it can suggest that you can't handle your obligations and find balance. None of these outcomes are great in the workplace or in friendship groups.

At the risk of sounding like Oprah, we all get 168 hours a week. I get 168 hours, you get 168 hours, everybody gets 168 hours. I'll be the first to admit that there are people who accomplish far more than me in their 168 hours. Certainly, those people are busier than me, and I'm busier than some people. You're probably in the same boat. We can't all be too busy, can we? How does this change when we look at our use of time with intentionality?

How: You get 168 hours. How you spend them is up to you. For a great treatise on this, check out Laura Vanderkam's book *168 Hours: You Have More Time Than You Think*. Just like the title, you do have more time than you think. Most of us are really good at wasting time. The internet in general can be a rabbit hole of good intentions but an unplanned time expenditure. While Vanderkam expands on this far better than I will here, the gist of it is this: allow your values to inform your priorities, and allow your priorities to inform your use of time.

What happens when, instead of a default answer of "I'm so busy," you bring an attitude of curiosity to the moments triggering your "too busy" urge? This may allow you to fully understand what you are feeling when you say "busy." You can then communicate more accurately and honestly to others, and most importantly, to yourself. Does "too busy" to you signify "my life is out of balance" or "I've bitten off more than I can chew?" If so, maybe that's worth paying attention to, rather than glossing it over under the guise of "too busy." What is your intention when communicating to others that you are "too busy?" Do you want them to help you? Are you one-upping them, feeling you fall short if you can't compete? Are you wary of more responsibilities being thrust upon you so you end-run the anticipated request with a "too busy" response? Deep and honest self-reflection may be required to gain insight into your motivations.

If you're doing too much and want help, you could directly ask for assistance. If you don't want added responsibility, you could wait for it to be asked of you and then kindly reply, "I'm working hard to be balanced in my use of time, and I know right now is not a good time for me to take on another responsibility. But I'm flattered that you considered me for this task." If you want to one-up them, maybe this requires some thought about how you are filling your own tank and sense of worth, because filling it at the expense of others is probably not a sustainable strategy.

Reflection and Implementation Tool

My main takeaways from this chapter:

My goal to use this in my own life:

Specific opportunities I may have to use this strategy or skill:

Obstacles to using this skill and meeting this goal:

Reflection and Implementation Tool

How to problem solve these obstacles

My commitment to use this skill (rate 0-10):

After implementation, here is my reflection on how this worked for me:

Raindrop moments where I can use this skill in the future:

Section 4: Mindfulness and the Art of Living

Chapter 33: Compassionate Connection

What: Deepen your connections through practicing compassion.

Why: As a society, we are digitally connected more than ever. In minutes, I can find my grade school classmates' digital fingerprints online and reach out to them. I can send a text message to a friend in southeast Asia, and she can respond seconds later. I can replace handwritten letters with emails that are simultaneously sent to my entire holiday card list. So, why are we all feeling so disconnected?

In a recent survey conducted by Cigna (you can read the analysis on NPR's public health topics from May 2018), nearly 50% of Americans reported that they feel alone or left out sometimes or always. Perhaps even more concerning, younger people who have grown up largely "digitally connected" are at the highest risk for loneliness, with the greatest percentage of lonely respondents coming from Gen Z (born mid 1990s to early 2000s). What's more, loneliness is correlated with a large number of physical health concerns in addition to depression and suicidal ideation.

So why are we virtually connected but feeling so disconnected? Human beings evolved over hundreds of thousands of years as extremely social creatures, dependent on others for survival. Our DNA is coded with a need to connect with other flesh and blood human beings. One example: oxytocin, the "feel good" hormone, is released with human contact. In addition to providing us with a burst of positive feelings, oxytocin performs protective functions on the cardiac muscle. In other words, giving and receiving hugs doesn't just feel good. Hugs are good for your heart. Such a sophisticated interplay of social connection leading to physical wellness suggests that evolution favored individuals with a higher level of connection.

How: Increasing connections--real life, physical connection--is the antidote to loneliness. But these aren't your run of the mill "hey how are you, I'm fine, have a nice day," interactions you may have with a shop clerk. Or the work focused interactions you may have with coworkers. We need deep and rich connections with people who care about us, and whom we care about. If you don't have that in your life, you are not alone, as the statistics on loneliness tell us. It takes work to form these connections, and may require pushing yourself out of your comfort zone to find such opportunities.

I am a big fan of yoga, and one of my favorite parts of a yoga practice is ending practice with "Namaste." Literally translated as "I bow to you," this phrase signifies an appreciation of, and identification with, the good in others. By meeting others in a space where we see their good and connect that to our good, while they connect with ours as well, we are momentarily connected in community. Taken off the yoga mat, compassionate connection entails seeing people without judgement, looking for the good in others, and finding the common human experiences that connect us all. Sure, this can happen in brief exchanges in a shop, but richer connections come through community.

If you're looking to increase connection, think of the communities to which you already belong. The workplace, extended family, your neighborhood, a fitness center, a religious institution, community "hubs" such as libraries and recreation centers, and charitable or volunteer organizations are all opportunities for rich, compassionate connections. If you have these connections, seek to deepen them. Get more involved, share more of your true self, and make efforts to know others in a deeper way. If you don't have these connections, find them. Your interests and passions may be a starting point.

Find a group with similar interests, beliefs, and ideals, and you're likely to find your community. Virtual connections can also be rich and meaningful, often leading to in-person connections if geography is not a barrier. Just manage your search for true connection while balancing the surface level connection that can be pulled through social media.

Reflection and Implementation Tool

My main takeaways from this chapter:

My goal to use this in my own life:

Specific opportunities I may have to use this strategy or skill:

Obstacles to using this skill and meeting this goal:

Reflection and Implementation Tool

How to problem solve these obstacles

My commitment to use this skill (rate 0-10):

After implementation, here is my reflection on how this worked for me:

Raindrop moments where I can use this skill in the future:

Chapter 34: Mindful Management

What: Skip the heavy-handed managing and listen mindfully to your employees if you want to see performance improve.

Why: If you manage any employees, or quite honestly, if your management responsibilities include a domestic partner and small people, you more than likely give feedback to your people from time to time. Performance reviews can be an extremely stressful situation for many, resulting in acute anxiety and fear reactions in some. Stressful situations do not set the brain up to utilize feedback in a helpful manner, but rather lead to scenarios of defensiveness. In the workplace, this can lead to people clinging to their former ways, blaming others, or feeling over-managed and stifled by their boss.

Itzchakov and Kluger studied the listening styles of managers during performance feedback situations and the impact on employee stress and attitude. You can read more details about their findings in the Harvard Business Review's May 2018 online archives. In a nutshell, they found that when listeners were using their "best listening skills" (asking questions and reflecting), speakers felt lower levels of stress and social anxiety, and were more able to reflect on their own strengths and weaknesses. "Poor listeners" (distracted listeners) led to higher levels of stress and a speaker's decreased ability to reflect on positives and negatives.

If you're reading this, my guess is that you want your direct reports to feel heard, appreciated, and empowered to reflect honestly on strengths and weaknesses. If they can do this effectively, they will identify their own areas of need or growth and be open to collaborating with you on how to reach these goals. You've likely heard of the criticism sandwich (use positives to start and end, with criticism in the middle of the sandwich), so why not move to a mindful listening based reflection sandwich?

How: Use your best mindful listening skills when conducting performance reviews and giving feedback. You can even start practicing in any listening situation. To bring these specific techniques to a performance review situation, you will likely need to prompt your direct reports with some instructions to reflect on areas of growth and challenge over the reporting period. You might prompt them first to share an area of growth, strength, success, or pride. Listen with attention, clarify as needed, and reflect what you are hearing and the emotions and growth behind the situations shared.

Next, move into an area of challenge, difficulty, or struggle. This is where you may need to bite your tongue and really use your mindful listening skills to be present without jumping into problem solving mode. You can guide gently but your role is to reflect, clarify, and allow a level of trust to develop that your employee/partner/child can share openly and honestly, in order for them to problem solve this with your support but without your direct intervention.

Close the discussion with a return to positive focus, perhaps with a reflection on future goals, or bridging from an area of strength to support an area of challenge. Following this model, you may end the conversation with deeper rapport, a better understanding of this person, and a more motivated and self-empowered individual.

Reflection and Implementation Tool

My main takeaways from this chapter:

My goal to use this in my own life:

Specific opportunities I may have to use this strategy or skill:

Obstacles to using this skill and meeting this goal:

Reflection and Implementation Tool

How to problem solve these obstacles

....

....

....

My commitment to use this skill (rate 0-10):

....

....

....

After implementation, here is my reflection on how this worked for me:

....

....

....

Raindrop moments where I can use this skill in the future:

....

....

....

Chapter 35: Mindful Mailing

What: Increase your awareness and intentionality around use of email.

Why: Here are some numbers to consider: 4 - the number of email accounts I need to check, 567-the number of emails currently sitting in the "in" box of my most-used work email account, 1138 - the number of emails currently in the "junk" folder of my "personal" email account. It becomes overwhelming. The inboxes get managed as I'm able, but more and more, I'm finding that I think I've responded to an email when I've actually "mentally responded" but not *actually* sent an email. The reason? Divided attention.

We like to think we can multitask, but research again and again shows us that our brains are not optimized for multitasking. We do much better when we can give full attention to one task at a time. Our brains are not windows operating systems, but our technology treats us as if we can move quickly and seamlessly between multiple points of attention. Constantly pinging, vibrating, and chirping, our phones, watches, and laptops remind us every time the outside world wants space across our limited attention span. Not only are we constantly pulled away from whatever we are involved in, but we are pulled to respond when we are not necessarily in the optimal mental and physical environments to respond. The result is exhaustion, stress, and a sense that the work day never ends. Time to be mindful of our email use.

How: New York's got it right. A bill has been introduced to the NYC legislature to ban work requirements forcing employees to be available by email after work hours. I'm not sure we need legislation for this to happen, but I like the mindset behind it. Until laws are passed, here's a little secret: you get to set the boundary on when and how you respond to emails. Just because your phone registers a new message, you don't have to read it nor respond to it.

Easier said than done? Try this. Look at your calendar for the day. Make an educated guess at how much time reading and responding to email should take you. Divide that time into two or three chunks, and schedule it during your day. Try the experiment of only looking at and responding to email during that time. When you are working on emails, try to stay totally focused on reading and responding to emails. As you come across junk, take the 30 seconds needed to unsubscribe from lists. Your future self will thank you. And track how long email takes. If you've set aside twenty minutes but it really only takes five, that's information that will help you with scheduling and may change your mindset. If you spend much longer on email than you anticipate, that could explain your stress level, and help you plan your day in a more informed way.

If your job is heavily dependent on email, you may need to work around the parameters of this to make it reasonable. You might consider using an auto reply, stating you check emails at scheduled times throughout the day, and that anyone with an urgent issue should call you. Shutting down notifications on your phone, watch, or fitness band can also help reduce the temptation to be sucked into emails. Increased mindfulness on how you use email and set parameters around it may allow you to focus more fully on all tasks.

Reflection and Implementation Tool

My main takeaways from this chapter:

My goal to use this in my own life:

Specific opportunities I may have to use this strategy or skill:

Obstacles to using this skill and meeting this goal:

Reflection and Implementation Tool

How to problem solve these obstacles

My commitment to use this skill (rate 0-10):

After implementation, here is my reflection on how this worked for me:

Raindrop moments where I can use this skill in the future:

Chapter 36: Getting Un-Busy

What: Decrease your "busy" so that your mind can move into the state of calm which is conducive to creative problem solving.

Why: As a society, we have a major busyness problem. Let's examine our addiction to being busy. We often choose to inhabit a space of constant stimulation, and then project that appearance and expectation to those around us.

Why would we want to be sending out the "look how busy I am signal"? Some of you probably read that and laughed out loud. You know too well that busyness is rewarded in the workforce and in society at large. It signals dedication, perseverance, and success. As a social species, we use signaling behavior to let others know our place in the group. In that respect, we're not that much different from apes or a pack of dogs. However, we have a choice in this matter and we don't have to subscribe to "busy is best." We can choose to decrease our busy addiction, be intentional in our signaling, and not reinforce busyness as a value in our communities. Some corporate cultures are moving away from the idea that busy means better employees, moving to an increased time off model to allow employees to really disconnect and refresh. But even without specific external support to recharge, we can continue to strive to be less busy and more present in our work and personal lives.

How: I've already suggested earlier that we experiment with shutting down notifications and containing the time spent on potential distractions, such as reading and responding to email, texts, tweets, and other social media. In addition to decreasing the addicting and distracting pull of technology, scheduling specific times to check email or surf the web also frees up our schedules to be intentional about creative planning time.

We've probably all had the experience of trying to find a solution to a problem but struggling to come up with ideas. Later on, when we aren't even thinking about the issue, like magic a solution pops into our mind. It's not really magic; we maintain awareness of those items our brains are consciously managing. This includes topics we're thinking about, talking about, working through, the 80s hit we're singing to ourselves, and whatever else is taking up space in our heads. In addition to this, our brain is processing all kinds of information by connecting new information to previously learned information and stored memories. These new connections form synapses between brain cells (though structurally different, you might think of them as bridges), creating an unimaginably rich and dense neural network. Give the ol' noggin enough time, and eventually a couple of brain cells connect and, Eureka! you've solved your problem.

This doesn't always happen on demand. We need time and opportunities to play creatively with knowledge in order to form these connections. Ever had a great idea in the shower? You're not alone. Guess what doesn't happen in the shower? Interruption, email, phone calls, lost socks that need to be found... you get the idea. Minimize those distractions and recreate your shower environment when you need to problem solve. Perhaps go for a walk outside of the office, grab a notepad or your dry erase markers and sequester yourself in the conference room, or otherwise shut down the outside world for a bit. Draw or doodle--either about your problem or just to get some creative energy flowing. (Check out Zen tangles if you want to learn a new way to let your brain play through doodling.) When your brain can relax during intentional creative time, you'll be amazed at the ideas it can generate. Your job is to give it the space, manage the interruptions, and bring an attitude of patience and curiosity to the process.

Reflection and Implementation Tool

My main takeaways from this chapter:

_____

_____

_____

My goal to use this in my own life:

_____

_____

_____

Specific opportunities I may have to use this strategy or skill:

_____

_____

_____

Obstacles to using this skill and meeting this goal:

_____

_____

_____

Reflection and Implementation Tool

How to problem solve these obstacles

_____

_____

_____

My commitment to use this skill (rate 0-10):

_____

_____

_____

After implementation, here is my reflection on how this worked for me:

_____

_____

_____

Raindrop moments where I can use this skill in the future:

_____

_____

_____

Chapter 37: Elastic Thinking

What: Free up your brain to think outside the box... and around the box... and under the box... and through the box.

Why: Leonard Mlodinow writes of a new set of talents needed for success in an ever changing workforce in his book *Elastic: Flexible Thinking in a Time of Change.*

He coined the term "elastic thinking" to denote the skill set that allows a person to look beyond and challenge the conventional assumptions, opening themselves up to new ideas and paradigms. These elastic thinkers are comfortable dwelling in a land of ambiguity and contradiction, trusting that, with time, their brain will reach a different understanding or awareness that will lead to growth and problem solving.

We've already touched on the idea of "unbusying" our brains in order to let them work through problems and think creatively. Elastic thought similarly benefits from uncluttered mental space for thoughts and ideas to percolate. Time pressure and immediate deadlines doom elastic thought to a quick and premature death. Mlodinow describes ideas as generating in the subconscious or preconscious mind. Under the pressure of time, the more novel and "far out" ideas are filtered by what he calls the brain's "executive." Think strict boss who doesn't have time to consider your wild ideas and out of the box thinking. However, providing the brain with time to muse and create in the absence of deadlines, excessive sensory stimuli, and distractions (cell phones), allows these ideas to fully form and present themselves coherently to our conscious awareness. As we've already explored, those great ideas that you have in the shower, or while exercising? No small coincidence. Let's turn towards intentional practices to allow for elastic thought.

How: Mindfully informed focus can be your friend if you are trying to problem solve in novel ways. By bringing mindful attention to the present moment without judgment, we free up our brain to let go of assumption, expectation, and "rules." Thus freed, our brain can entertain far out ideas that are *so crazy, they just might work.* When we are mindfully aware, judgments, such as an idea being wrong or right, go out the window. In these judgement-free spaces, ideas are free to present themselves just as they are. What we do with them is up to us.

You might work on using mindful awareness to increase your elastic thinking by applying this exercise to your next problem-solving session. Gather all the information you have about the issue or situation. Bring your awareness to the difficulty without focusing on what has worked or not worked in the past. Give your brain access to all the known facts about the situation or problem. If this is a joint venture, allow your team to do the same. Provide time to let these thoughts work in the brain's back channels. To use a computer analogy, consider yourself as minimizing the window on the issue, rather than closing the program. Perhaps set a date several days or a week later to revisit the topic. In the meantime, go about your work.

Periodically throughout the "wait time," practice a focused meditation on the issue at hand. Center on breath awareness, then move into a guided visualization in which you watch your thoughts about the problem move through your head without judgement. I love to use the image of a movie screen, where we can watch thoughts play out on the screen without engaging with them as they move from one side of the screen to the other.

After your meditation and visualization, write down every idea that presents itself to you. Don't think about whether it will work or whether has been tried already; just write them all down. Immerse yourself in these exercises over a period of time, bringing ideas back to the hive-mind of your teammates if you are working in a group. As ideas are shared, take them back to your own space and continue this process. You might be surprised at what presents itself once you drop the need to fit within what you already know, and give your brain the time it needs for creative expression.

Reflection and Implementation Tool

My main takeaways from this chapter:

My goal to use this in my own life:

Specific opportunities I may have to use this strategy or skill:

Obstacles to using this skill and meeting this goal:

Reflection and Implementation Tool

How to problem solve these obstacles

My commitment to use this skill (rate 0-10):

After implementation, here is my reflection on how this worked for me:

Raindrop moments where I can use this skill in the future:

Chapter 38: Mindful Listening

What: Non-judging awareness of perspectives cultivates empathy and leads to leadership success.

Why: Great leaders have the ability to see what others do not see, writes Harvard Business Review (April 2018) columnist Bill Taylor. He describes a business leadership program that brings together people from diverse skill sets to discuss art. If there is anything that will evoke a variety of perspectives and interpretations, it's art. Imagine being paired with someone very different from yourself and being asked to describe a work of art, then listening to this partner describe the same work of art from a very different perspective. Being able to truly listen and consider these other perspectives is the root of empathy and compassion.

Staying within "what we know" has serious consequences. In business, failure to think creatively leads to limited growth and new idea generation. Bring in diverse ideas and you create an environment rich in the building blocks of innovation: ideas from various perspectives coming together to generate something larger and meet needs in new and imaginative ways.

How: While Taylor describes programs that bring people together over art, you can pick any topic to stretch your listening skills. Mindful listening requires us to drop the mantle of prior expectation and experiences in order to hear the speaker without judgments, without concern about how the speaker's ideas intersect with our own belief systems. Imagine hearing someone and considering their ideas and thoughts as if you have never heard anything quite like them before. This is what mindfulness writers refer to as "beginner's mind."

We are all guilty of hearing portions of what a speaker says then jumping quickly to a mental rehearsal of our rebuttal. As soon as we mentally leave the conversation to focus on our own response, we have lost our mindful presence and we are no longer deeply listening to the speaker. You can practice bringing mindful awareness to others any time you are in a conversation by working on bringing your full attention to the speaker without judging what he or she is saying or the merit of the ideas he or she is expressing. You can reinforce this by using clarification. After the speaker finishes presenting their idea, repeat back what you understood and ask the speaker to correct anything that you may have misunderstood.

Next, take the time to thoughtfully consider what the speaker has said before making any response, whether they are suggesting a pizza with extra anchovies for lunch, or a new packaging solution for your product that will initially create additional investment but lead to savings over time. Use these skills frequently in all conversations to sharpen your ability. You can also practice a response that communicates that you need time to thoughtfully consider these other perspectives ("Thank you for sharing that. I need to take some time to reflect on this and the way your ideas would work in conjunction with XYZ"). Then, invite others to hear your ideas and collaborate on integrating them.

Reflection and Implementation Tool

My main takeaways from this chapter:

My goal to use this in my own life:

Specific opportunities I may have to use this strategy or skill:

Obstacles to using this skill and meeting this goal:

Reflection and Implementation Tool

How to problem solve these obstacles

My commitment to use this skill (rate 0-10):

After implementation, here is my reflection on how this worked for me:

Raindrop moments where I can use this skill in the future:

Chapter 39: Examine the Weeds

What: Rather than ripping out the weeds that sprout in your life, why not examine them first?

Why: I love being in a well-tended garden in full bloom. By late-spring, my garden has been weeded, mulched, fertilized, watered, watered, watered, and begins to show the rewards. But there's a skinny area of my garden that gets intense sun with a southern exposure, is situated on a dry slope, and is bordered by concrete that reflects the intense sun. I've lost plenty of expensive plants in that patch of soil.

One year an interesting looking weed sprung up in that difficult slice of garden. It didn't look like most of the weeds that come up in my garden, so I let it be for a bit to see if it would identify itself. Sure enough, it turned out to be a sunflower. But not just any sunflower; it was a variety with one thick stalk and a myriad of two-to-three-inch diameter flower heads. Towards the end of the summer, I counted over 100 blossoms and buds from that single stalk. Sure glad I let that weed stay! A bird likely grabbed too many seeds to carry from my bird feeder, dropped one in the perfect spot, and that sunflower grew and grew and grew.

Those many seed heads set out many, many seeds. The following year, I had so many sunflowers coming up in my little garden area! As hard as it is to grow other plants there, I did have some perennials that were thriving, and I couldn't let them be overshadowed by the sunflower forest. I weeded down to about 5 sunflowers--healthy seedlings growing where I most wanted them. Many seeds had sprouted along my neighbor's driveway and I left them (not my property, right?). The plants in my neighbor's verge developed into a thick forest of spindly plants topping out at two feet and succumbing to heat. My five or so plants towered to about 6 feet tall, with a variety of different single- and multi-flowered heads.

What's the moral here? Let a weed grow now and then. It might be something you love. And because it picked its own spot to grow, and grew without you tending it, you know it has the strength to live without coddling. But let too many weeds grow and they will all compete for the same resources, resulting in a forest of spindly seedlings that succumb to the summer heat. Starting to see where I'm going with all this?

How: Turn mindful attention to the "weeds" of your life, the ideas, projects, relationships, and emotions that crop up (no pun intended) without your active cultivation. We tend to squash those, right? I don't have time for that, that person is too draining to spend time with, I don't like feeling this way. You may have heard the expression "what we resist, persists." Rather than squashing them down, turn towards these with acceptance and curiosity. What might they be teaching you? If they keep coming back, you know they're important.

Conversely, don't let the weeds completely take over. Even if they are beautiful, too many will divert your attention and focus, steal all your resources, and result in stress and overwhelm. Use your mindful attention and awareness to decide which of these projects, ideas, relationships, etc. are in alignment with your current goals. It can be easy to get "shiny object syndrome" and chase after new idea after new idea (believe me, I'm a shiny object sufferer myself).

I love keeping an idea journal handy to capture whatever "weedy" energy is coming my way about a project, or ideas for how to progress on a project that is still in the dream stage. The act of writing it down helps gel the idea in memory as well as provides a reference point to return to when I'm ready to take the project on. The act of writing down the ideas and the development process, can also illuminate viable ideas that are aligned with my current goals, versus ideas that are too far off track and would be a pretty distraction rather than a goal-aligned pursuit. Capturing and containing the energy of these new ideas also allows the mind to stay focused more mindfully on the tasks at hand. Grab a notebook or journal to dedicate as your idea journal, and pair it up with whatever writing instruments make you the happiest. Periodically review ideas, note the ones that continue to resurface, and see what new connections begin to form. As your ideas gain steam, you might have individual notebooks or tabbed dividers for work ideas, household ideas, creative dreams, or whatever other weeds you'd like to cultivate.

Who knows? You might just find a sunflower in there.

Reflection and Implementation Tool

My main takeaways from this chapter:

My goal to use this in my own life:

Specific opportunities I may have to use this strategy or skill:

Obstacles to using this skill and meeting this goal:

Reflection and Implementation Tool

How to problem solve these obstacles

My commitment to use this skill (rate 0-10):

After implementation, here is my reflection on how this worked for me:

Raindrop moments where I can use this skill in the future:

Chapter 40: Mindful Traditions

What: Make intentional, value-informed decisions about traditions so they serve you and NOT the other way around.

Why: Ah, the holidays. We mark time as the earth continues its path around the sun by these dates imbued with special meaning. Religious days, cultural traditions, celebrations of birth--we share those days with those closest to us and draw on rituals of years past as part of the festivities.

The anticipation and expectation of traditions allows our brain to go into an autopilot mode. During times of potential stress, we know what is coming up next. In other words, our brain can say, "yes, I know this, it's familiar to me and safe." This gives structure, consistency, and predictability to the great unknown: the future. Our limbic system can exhale and settle into rest mode. Holiday celebrations and traditions allow us to connect in meaningful ways to the people with whom we are closest. This satisfies the parts of our brain that are motivated by human connection, a crucial need from a biological standpoint. These traditions keep us connected, and connected, for early humans at least, means survival of the group.

But all is not well in the land of tradition, and if we're not careful, our limbic system gets fired back up. No longer "needing" social connection for protection, our traditions have become embellished with the trappings of capitalism. Many traditions have become overwhelming and create a complicated set of rules leading to resource stress: your time, finances, and emotional bandwidth become taxed and you turn into a tradition automaton. Using mindful attention and allowing your values to inform your choices, you can take back the reins and show traditions who's the boss.

How: Think of an upcoming tradition-filled event in your life, or reflect on a past one. Close your eyes and develop a rich image of the past or anticipated event. What do you see, hear, taste, smell, feel? What emotions and thoughts arise? Stay connected to those images and notice any overlay of judgment by your mind. For now, simply label those judgments. Stay connected to the scene and the emotions, noting both positive and negative emotions.

Now open your eyes and create two lists: what you loved and what you disliked about the tradition. Start looking for common threads: perhaps the people involved, the scale (number of people, level of formality, etc.), the location(s), the expense, and anything else that surfaces. Look for common expressions of values. Those things that you really love probably connect somehow to the values you cherish. Those things that you hate probably don't light up your value system, and some may run counter to what you hold nearest and dearest.

Having identified your values related to this event, start circling the behaviors or aspects of the tradition that are most important to you and that you'd like to keep, while identifying the pieces to let go of. Close your eyes again, this time imagining your newly crafted tradition and what it would look, sound, smell, taste, and feel like. Notice your thoughts, emotions, and judgments. You've crafted your intentional tradition: that's step one.

Step two is talking to those people nearest and dearest to you about your desires. No, life is not perfect and hopefully we've all learned that we are not the center of the universe. Traditions are social constructs involving multiple people. Those other people may have some very different ideas about the importance of aspects of tradition than you do. And that's ok. The key is to have a rich, nonjudgmental conversation about your wants and needs, while listening to the desires of those around you. With some understanding of why a particular aspect is important to someone else, perhaps you'll choose to incorporate that into your ideal expression of the tradition. With heartfelt and intentional communication from you, those around you may better understand why you would like to alter traditions the way you do.

Are you saying "too little, too late?" Did you just drag yourself kicking and screaming through a month of holiday build up and now, exhausted and depleted, you're holding on by your fingernails to make it into a new year? Never fear. You can still apply this now. But you can also take a moment while these memories are freshest to notice and attend to your thoughts and feelings about what made for or detracted from a joyful holiday season. Jot down those traditions you want to continue, as well as the ones to scrap, and clip them to November of next year in your calendar. Your future self will thank you.

Reflection and Implementation Tool

My main takeaways from this chapter:

My goal to use this in my own life:

Specific opportunities I may have to use this strategy or skill:

Obstacles to using this skill and meeting this goal:

Reflection and Implementation Tool

How to problem solve these obstacles

My commitment to use this skill (rate 0-10):

After implementation, here is my reflection on how this worked for me:

Raindrop moments where I can use this skill in the future:

Chapter 41: Mindful Daybreak

What: Start the day with mindful awareness, setting the course of your day with intentionality.

Why: I am not a morning person. Chances are good that you are not a morning person either. Sources suggest that about 80% of the population are intermediates--neither early birds nor night owls, sometimes referred to as "hummingbirds", who base their wake/sleep cycle on the light levels. The remaining 20% is split between the early risers and the midnight-oil-burners, meaning that, in actuality, a very small percentage of people are true "larks", up and productive before the sun crests the horizon.

But society favors the early bird and much of our workaday clock is set around getting up early and grabbing the day by the horns. I don't love the idea of living a day that HAS horns which need grabbing, to be honest. Some communities are making changes towards evening the playing field for teens, with high school start times in many communities being pushed to a later morning start. If you're in the working world, or have small ones to prepare for the school day, you may not have any ability to dictate your start time, and working backwards from "go time" means getting up several hours earlier to get yourself ready and get children where they need to be before the bell rings.

We may not be able to change the clocks around us, but we can change a small part within ourselves and greet the day with mindful intention: free of judgments and present to witness and acknowledge ourselves just as we are in the moment.

How: Take a hard look at how your morning starts. What awakens you in the morning? What are your first actions? What is your relationship to the morning like, and how do you express this in your thoughts? Are you awakened by a harsh alarm clock, do you hit snooze for nine more minutes of fitful sleep then drag yourself wearily to the shower, accompanied by thoughts of how many more work days there are in the week until you can sleep in on the weekend? I've been there, and I know firsthand, that's no way to set the tone for the day.

Bringing your awareness to how your morning starts, try identifying three or four key parts of the morning where you can institute small, mindful changes. It could be as simple as taking a minute to breathe mindfully (that's about 7 breath cycles) upon sitting up but before you get out of bed. As you breathe, let your focus go to feeling and accepting whatever is going on in your body right now. Acknowledge those feelings and see what happens. You may find that, once acknowledged, discomfort lessens. Maybe you open your drapes or blinds immediately so that the morning light can help you awaken. If decision making is hard for you in the morning, you might try prepping everything in the evening: breakfast, lunch, clothes, and items you need for the day. Perhaps you'll land on a word to set the tone for your day, and return your attention to this intention throughout the morning until your brain naturally awakens.

Many people have great success by using formal meditation, either seated or during a brief yoga or walking meditation practice, to set intentions and prepare for the day. If you can carve out five to ten minutes, you might give this a try, perhaps as your coffee or tea brews. You can find lots of brief guided meditations for free with the Insight Timer app. Whatever you try, give it at least a couple of weeks before judging whether it has been helpful or not, and give it at least a month of consistent practice to make it a habit.

Reflection and Implementation Tool

My main takeaways from this chapter:

My goal to use this in my own life:

Specific opportunities I may have to use this strategy or skill:

Obstacles to using this skill and meeting this goal:

Reflection and Implementation Tool

How to problem solve these obstacles

My commitment to use this skill (rate 0-10):

After implementation, here is my reflection on how this worked for me:

Raindrop moments where I can use this skill in the future:

Chapter 42: Mindful Evenings

What: Rather than racing to the finish line of the day and feeling frustrated when you don't automatically fall asleep, set yourself up for Zzzzs with some mindful awareness.

Why: Ever fall into bed, exhausted from the day, but your mind is still racing through the day's activities and problem solving whatever real or imagined problems presented themselves? You're not alone. According to the Cleveland Clinic, about 50% of adults are plagued by occasional insomnia, with 10% experiencing chronic insomnia, defined as trouble sleeping three or more days per week for at least a month.

The average adult spends about one-third of their life asleep, but have you given much thought to the importance of sleep? Sleep allows us our brain to do a deep-cleaning from the day and consolidate new memory while the body rests and engages in cellular repair. We store energy, save energy, and move newly learned material into accessible storage while slumbering. The right quantity and quality of sleep also sets us up for positive mood the following day, and for the alertness we need for new learning and problem solving.

If you don't give much thought to sleep until you switch off the night table lamp, you may want to back up a bit. Sleep hygiene strategies refer to all the things we do during the day to set ourselves up for a good night's sleep. They include such things as creating the ideal sleep environment: quiet, dark, slightly cooler than the daytime, and without distractions. Our body is prepped for sleep when we are careful to exercise daily but not right before bed, avoid caffeine late in the day, avoid heavy meals before bed, and monitor the impact of any drug or alcohol use on our sleep. Behaviors engaged in during the day also contribute to sleep hygiene. Seeking out early exposure to light, avoidance of daytime napping, decreasing light levels through the early evening and avoidance of bright light in the hours before bed, and restricting the bedroom for sleep and intimacy make the list of behavioral strategies for good sleep.

One final strategy to help with sleep is a consistent and calming bedtime routine. If you've cared for a baby or younger child, you probably know the importance of bedtime routines: cuddling in a rocking chair with a bottle, reading books (often the same ones) together, quiet music, low lights, and a transition into bed. No wonder we say they "sleep like babies." Want the same for you? Then bring mindful awareness to your bedtime routine.

How: Begin to view the hour or so before bed as sacred time. This may be a big shift if you are the type of person who schedules every last minute out of the day, perhaps saving the quiet nighttime hours for uninterrupted work. Do yourself a favor and consciously notice your tendencies, thoughts, and urges for the time leading up to bed. Does your current strategy work well for you? Are there areas for improvement? As you notice your typical approach to bedtime and routine, notice what works well, what may not work well but needs to be done at some point during the day, and what no longer serves you. Keep the good, move the things that need to happen but interfere with sleep to an earlier time slot, and (if possible) scrap those behaviors that interfere with your sleep.

You might approach the period of time leading up to bed as an opportunity to build a thoughtful and intentioned routine, including all the behaviors and experiences that help you to fall asleep. Formal meditation practice, however brief, might be a part of this time period. You might also find guided relaxation exercises, gentle yoga practices, or stretching exercises that help your mind and body to relax.

Quieting your mind is another way to prepare for bed. Writing is one way to "empty" thoughts from intangible neural-sparking to ink on paper. Containing thoughts in such a manner can help you to put them to rest for the evening so that they don't consume your mind while you try to sleep. You could try listing out your to-do list for tomorrow, containing all the nagging "don't forget" thoughts in your head. You could also reflect on the day, either through writing or a mindful remembering process, wherein you walk through your day in your head and observe moments of strong emotion, sensation, judgment, curiosity, attention, distraction, etc. (For more journaling suggestions, see Chapter 46.)

With mind and body relaxed, move into the routine part of your bedtime preparation. This could be engaging in physical hygiene activities, a routine sweep through the house to lock doors and settle people and pets for the night, listening to quiet music, engaging in a quiet activity that helps you relax like reading, crafts, a jigsaw puzzle, or doodling. Avoid electronics during this time for two reasons. The light directly to your eyes interferes with your brain's ability to judge that it is bedtime, decreasing melatonin production. Secondly, the content of email, social media, and online news is often the opposite of relaxing, revving up and engaging a mind that is trying to prepare for sleep.

The bedtime routine, by virtue of being a routine, signals to the brain that sleep is coming soon. In behavioral terms, each activity that we engage in before bed (brushing teeth, showering, reading a book in bed) becomes a classically conditioned stimulus, or a "cue", that sleep is coming soon. As these activities or cues occur, we become sleepier, right up until the time we shut off the light and drop off to sleep. Bring full mindful attention to these cue activities in the bedtime routine to take advantage of their sleep-inducing powers.

Trouble dropping off to sleep? As frustrating as this can be, this is an opportunity to notice the judging mind and again try to bring non-judgmental awareness to the experience. Maybe you notice a lot of thoughts about inability to fall asleep.

Can you notice those thoughts without engaging with them? Can you return to the present moment, the bed and room around you, the sensations in your body, as opposed to inhabiting the imagined future and worries about what a poor night's sleep might mean for your next day? Perhaps this is a time to utilize mindful breathing, noticing each breath and counting it as "one" on the exhale (yes, every breath is one, a reminder that each is its own unique experience). Let go of the tendency to engage with thoughts about sleep and you may just find that you reach your goal with little effort at all.

Reflection and Implementation Tool

My main takeaways from this chapter:

My goal to use this in my own life:

Specific opportunities I may have to use this strategy or skill:

Obstacles to using this skill and meeting this goal:

Reflection and Implementation Tool

How to problem solve these obstacles

My commitment to use this skill (rate 0-10):

After implementation, here is my reflection on how this worked for me:

Raindrop moments where I can use this skill in the future:

Chapter 43: Mindful of Accomplishment

What: Train your brain to pay more attention to what you do, and frame your daily goals in reasonable "chunks," to feel the positive effects of achievement at the end of the day.

Why: Ever walk out of your office, or lay your head down on your pillow at night, with a sense that you really achieved what you set out to achieve that day? It's a great feeling of satisfaction that can improve mood and decrease our levels of stress and anxiety. Accomplishment provides a burst of dopamine in the brain, a major player in the motivational component of reward-motivated behavior. In other words, it just feels good to accomplish things.

However, our brain has a built in negative cognitive bias, which means we pay more attention to the negative than to the positive. Thus, we are more likely to remember and dwell on those tasks that were left incomplete, or tasks registered by our brain as "failures." This is a safety feature of our brain. By paying attention to the negative (for instance, a missing rung on a ladder or a hole in the ground), we are likely to keep ourselves physically safe. But in a world where physical safety is likely not a constant battle, paying attention to the negative (a report not finished, a basket of laundry left unfolded) doesn't necessarily help us, and may harm us by raising our stress levels over seemingly trivial tasks.

Fortunately, there are some easy ways to counter our brain's negative cognitive bias, starting with mindful attention and ending with setting and reflecting on reasonable and specific goals.

How: The first step is to look at the tasks you have set out for the day, whether these are at work or at home. Make a specific list. For any tasks taking more than a short amount of time, break them into steps and list every step towards completion. For example, rather than adding "write report" to your list, you might add "write outline, gather research, seek management approval, write initial draft, seek collegial feedback, write final draft." Once you have broken this multi-step task down into steps, you can be realistic about the amount of time each step will take and plan accordingly. Assign each of these steps mini-due dates and timelines and add them to your calendar and daily to-do lists. For instance, the outline might take from 9-10am, initial research could take two to three hours, with a management meeting scheduled for 3pm. Adding that specific timeline to your planner is more likely to result in actual accomplishment of the steps as well as a sense of achievement rather than overwhelm at a too-big task. This also encourages you to focus mindfully on these specific tasks for a specified time frame.

As you complete tasks on your daily list, try taking a quick moment of mindful awareness. Close your eyes and assess your feeling of accomplishment. Rate this from 1 to 5 and really notice how you experience these feelings. Jot down the number in your planner next to the task. After several days of doing this, you ought to see some patterns emerge: the types of activities that lead to a high or a low sense of accomplishment. Look for common themes, try to increase the activities that lead to accomplishment, and look for ways to frame the less accomplishment-inducing activities in a way that may help you to feel more accomplished. For instance, you might notice that you bit off more than you could chew on an activity, resulting in leaving it unfinished. No problem! Just schedule yourself a longer amount of time or break it down into several steps next time around.

The second step of feeling accomplishment is to bring mindful awareness to your day before retiring, whether that means leaving the office, finishing housework to pick up kids from school, or going to bed. Close your eyes and really focus on the day and notice what arises.

Bring your attention to both the things that were completed and the things that are yet to be finished. Now open your eyes and, if you haven't already, check off all those accomplishments in your calendar and bring awareness to the sense of accomplishment without judgment. For anything not completed or left undone, start another to-do list. That list can be your basis for your next day's goals. And if your brain tries to remind you later on about your unfinished tasks, you can gently remind it, "hey brain, that's on my list for tomorrow. Thanks for looking out for me, but I've got this handled." Your brain may continue to chatter at you about these tasks but you can direct your attention elsewhere and turn down the volume on this noise. When you don't attend to the worried thoughts, they will extinguish themselves over time.

Reflection and Implementation Tool

My main takeaways from this chapter:

My goal to use this in my own life:

Specific opportunities I may have to use this strategy or skill:

Obstacles to using this skill and meeting this goal:

Reflection and Implementation Tool

How to problem solve these obstacles

....

....

....

My commitment to use this skill (rate 0-10):

....

....

....

After implementation, here is my reflection on how this worked for me:

....

....

....

Raindrop moments where I can use this skill in the future:

....

....

....

Chapter 44: Wabi-Sabi: The Beauty in Imperfection and Impermanence

What: Tap into the Japanese concept of wabi-sabi to embrace the beautiful imperfections that surround you.

Why: Wabi-sabi is the Japanese aesthetic that in imperfection, impermanence, and incompleteness, we can find beauty. From what I have read, it is a concept that is a little difficult to translate into English and western culture, and perhaps the kind of thing that "you know when you see" if you have been deeply rooted in eastern culture. Translated literally, "wabi" is "rustic simplicity" or "understated elegance" and "sabi" is "finding pleasure in the imperfect."

Contrast that to what we are surrounded with in western culture: airbrushed models, products selling us the perfect image, and curated social media posts touting sculpted bodies and perfect lives. It's a little hard to reconcile this with wabi-sabi, and a little hard to remember the simple elegance in life when we are bombarded by gloss, plastic, and curation.

A return to the simpler things in life, an embracing of growth, and finding grace and love in the imperfect may be the perfect antidote.

How: You can incorporate a little wabi-sabi in any way you'd like in your life. To access this concept with mindfulness, you might choose to focus on noticing the imperfect, the growing and not yet complete, and the impermanent and fading around us. A mindful walk through nature is perhaps the perfect way to focus on these concepts. You'll rarely find a perfect tree; bark is marked with scars, a bird has drilled a hole halfway up the trunk, a branch may grow askew due to a nearby powerline or another obstacle. And yet we can find beauty (and shade!) under this imperfect tree's canopy. Streams and rivers are rarely perfect straight shots. They meander as a result of moving around obstacles over time. In fact, a measure of the age of a body of running water is how topsy turvy of a path it carves. With an eye to growth, change, and dissolution, bring your full awareness to the nature around you.

Another way to bring wabi-sabi into your awareness is through physical reminders within your sphere of existence. There is some comfort and connection to be found in the old, dog-eared reference book that has traveled with you from office to office over time. The favorite coffee mug with a chip in the side. The comfy cardigan sweater you no longer wear outside of the house but bundle in on a cold weekend day in front of the fireplace. These items embody more than their functionality. They are a tangible reminder of memories from your life. You can enjoy these items as they are, imperfect, fading, and (not to be overly dramatic) on their path back to dust, like all of us. They also serve as a physical connection to non-judgmentalism, to compassion towards all imperfect beings, and to the journey of birth, growth, and death that marks all of our lives.

Reflection and Implementation Tool

My main takeaways from this chapter:

My goal to use this in my own life:

Specific opportunities I may have to use this strategy or skill:

Obstacles to using this skill and meeting this goal:

Reflection and Implementation Tool

How to problem solve these obstacles

....

....

....

My commitment to use this skill (rate 0-10):

....

_____

....

After implementation, here is my reflection on how this worked for me:

_____

....

_____

Raindrop moments where I can use this skill in the future:

....

....

....

Chapter 45: Mindful Conflict

What: Notice your approach (or avoidance) of conflict and bring mindful awareness to the process

Why: Did you internally shudder when you saw the word "conflict"? If so, you're not alone. As a culture, we don't like conflict. The word brings to mind fights, arguments, one person winning and one person losing. We envision faces pinched in anger and insults hurled.

I had a wise fortune cookie recently that read "If you agree with your business partner on everything, you don't need a business partner." Let that really sink in for a bit. Conflict, at its purest form, is a difference of opinion. It is not the red-faced argument, the insults thrown, the win or the loss. It is a different perspective, one that challenges a previously held perspective.

How would your attitude towards conflict change if you could view it not as an impending argument but as an opportunity for growth and collaboration? Rather than avoiding conflict, you might view it as an unprecedented opportunity. My guess is that this is the exact attitude that allows visionaries to excel in their fields of work. But how do we move from viewing conflict as a bad thing to conflict as growth? It starts with mindful awareness of thoughts and a return to beginner's mind.

How: Beginner's mind is the idea that each thing that happens is brand new, such that we bring a level of attention, curiosity, and inquisitiveness to each experience *as if it never happened before*. Our brain loves to lump things into categories, whether they are physical objects, types of people, or abstract concepts. Through this rapid categorization, we are primed to respond to a new event based on our experience of seemingly similar events that occurred in the past. In that vein, we might hear a difference of opinions and the internal alarm bell starts to ring, "warning, fight ahead!" Our sympathetic nervous system then triggers the fight or flight response. In order to view a conflict as an opportunity, we first need to peel off all the layers of expectation and interpretation through the perspective of a beginner's mind, so that we don't trigger fight or flight and can remain present to a new experience in the here-and-now.

You might start by using the brain and body's signals as a warning sign. Perhaps you are in a meeting and you throw out an idea. A co-worker responds with "yeah, I don't think that will work. You're forgetting XYZ details and not accounting for budget. We should really stick with the game plan." Before responding, take a moment to stop and check in with yourself. Do you notice your heart rate rising, your face feeling flushed, tension in your large muscles? If you do, that's a sign that your fight or flight response is kicking in. Your body has sensed a threat and will respond with dukes up.

You might also notice changes in your thought process which signal that you are responding in a habitual way to a potential conflict. Bringing mindful awareness to your thoughts, you might recognize thoughts similar to, "Oh, here we go again. Joe always shoots down my ideas and sides with the boss. What a suck up!" Or, "Why can't my team ever support me? I ought to quit and work somewhere that would appreciate my ideas!" We tend to make a snap judgment (this situation is just like these other situations) and respond *as if we are in* that other situation, when, in reality, we are not. Each situation is unique. That's where the beginner's mind piece comes in to help you out.

Having identified by your body's response and your thought process that you are entering a perceived conflict, take a moment to break the mold of your past responses. Rather than riding the swelling wave of fight or flight physiology and habitual thought patterns, try to take a half step away and really observe. You might think "I'm noticing that my heart is beating fast, and I'm observing an urge to storm out of the conference room because I'm having thoughts that I am unappreciated." You might add, "Hmmm, that's interesting." Then bring some curiosity to the current situation. Be a scientist. You need to find evidence that your perceptions are accurate for your current situation.

A brief focus on breathing may turn around the physiological arousal, and allow you greater awareness so that you can take an attitude of inquisitiveness towards your thoughts. Once you can see your thoughts as habits of mind that may or may not apply to your current situation, you can look at your current situation with increased clarity. Maybe rather than reacting angrily to Joe CoWorker, you can just explore rather than react. "Joe, I'm curious to hear your thoughts on those details and how the budget would be impacted by what I propose." Totally different reaction, and one that would open the door to collaboration.

Can you invite-in conflict as opportunity in your life? If you turn towards conflict, with an attitude of curiosity and seeking a different understanding of the status quo, what doors will open for you?

Reflection and Implementation Tool

My main takeaways from this chapter:

My goal to use this in my own life:

Specific opportunities I may have to use this strategy or skill:

Obstacles to using this skill and meeting this goal:

Reflection and Implementation Tool

How to problem solve these obstacles

My commitment to use this skill (rate 0-10):

After implementation, here is my reflection on how this worked for me:

Raindrop moments where I can use this skill in the future:

Chapter 46: Mindful Journaling

What: Grab a pen and paper and bring present moment awareness to your thoughts.

Why: Find your mind frequently swirling? Lose track of what you were just thinking about doing? I have that experience almost every time that I sit down at my computer. I may grab my computer or phone with the intention of looking for something, and I'm almost immediately lost in whatever presents itself to me first (usually, social media). Then I find myself wondering what I was doing in the first place.

Journaling can be a helpful tool along the path to more mindful intentions. By bringing present moment awareness to our thoughts and deciding where we want to focus our thoughts, we help direct our behavior and choices.

Journaling has the added benefit of bringing motor action to thought through translating thought to words, to motion within the hands, and ultimately to streams of ink or graphite on paper that are meaningful. Writing allows for immediate reflection as we read what we've written, a process that removes us from our thoughts and provides a degree of objectivity that we may not always access. Even the process of curating thought to determine what portion is brought to the page allows for intentionality.

I can already hear some of you silently yelling objections in your head: I hate my writing! My hand cramps up! I'm much faster as a typist! Hey friends, I'm right there with you. While I don't hate my writing, my hand cramps up. If I write quickly it is illegible, and I can type much faster with readable results. My husband called me once from the store to ask why I had added "flamingos" to our grocery list. (It was tomatoes, right there with the lettuce and salsa for taco night, duh.)

When I stop and think about it, my messy, hasty writing is also a product of not being mindful--not allowing intentional creation of my product to inform my process. While my intention was to share my thoughts on what was needed for dinner through symbols that my partner could use at the store, my product was a sloppy mess that even I struggled to read. It created a funny anecdote but a useless shopping tool.

So, why not type it? Well, here's why. There is a growing pile of research that demonstrates that taking notes by hand, as opposed to through typing, results in better memory for the material written, better recall, and, for students, stronger test scores when tested on handwritten material. This is especially true for conceptual material; material that requires interaction with other knowledge for comprehension, as opposed to factual material that requires surface-level memorization.

Now, you're not being tested on your thoughts, but if they are worth thinking and considering, they may be worth remembering, interacting with, and processing at a deeper level. This process may bring you increased clarity, intentionality in goal setting, and reflection. Slowing down your writing so that you can produce a readable product will also provide an experience of mindful focus, with a byproduct of fewer unexpected flamingo purchases!

How: Set aside ten to fifteen minutes for this activity. You'll want to have some tools that will encourage and support you to write by hand. This may require a quick inventory of your paper and writing utensils. You could use a traditional journal, with or without lines, or simply a sheet of notebook paper. Some people prefer a larger page, while others are comfortable with a pocket-sized notebook. Whatever works for you, works for you. Whatever writing instrument allows you ease of writing and readable results is best. You can try different colored inks, perhaps for different days or different parts of your journaling process, pencil, or any variety of pen: gel ink, rollerball, fountain pen, ballpoint pen. If your hand cramps easily, look for a pen or pencil with a larger grip made from silicone, or experiment with adding grips to pens and pencils you already have.

There's really not much else to it; simply get your preferred tools and write. You could set a timer and write, just letting whatever thoughts you have become written word without censoring. This is sometimes referred to as a "morning pages" practice and can be a great tool to dump and organize thoughts before you start your day. You might go back to such journaling when you're done, with a different colored pen or highlighter and look for themes or items that will help you structure your day.

Others prefer a more structured way to journal, which can help to use your writing as a tool for reflection and goal setting. If this appeals to you, you might consider using a journal for what I'm dubbing a "5Gs" practice. Use this in the evening to reflect on the day and set intention for the morning. Use it in the morning to reflect on the prior day and set intention for the present day. Or split it between evening reflection and morning goal setting.

The 5Gs are Gratitude, Glad, Growth, Goals, and Let Go. Write three items for each category, and expand on each as much or as little as you want. This could take the form of five paragraphs, or five bulleted lists. Gratitude includes three times you were grateful or three things for which you are grateful. Glad signifies three things that went well during the day. Growth includes three opportunities that present you with room to grow and change. They could be three things that did not go well, or times when you didn't act with intentionality, which, on reflection, offer an opportunity to act differently in the future. Goals are areas of focus, which could be very specific to-do list items, or more general feeling and action states.

Finally, Let Go refers to those things that may be distressing to you but over which you have absolutely no control. They are worries without any opportunity for action. These are things that you can conceptualize as being released to the universe, being given to a Higher Power in prayer, or being put on paper to release them from space in your brain.

Reflection and Implementation Tool

My main takeaways from this chapter:

My goal to use this in my own life:

Specific opportunities I may have to use this strategy or skill:

Obstacles to using this skill and meeting this goal:

~ 221 ~

Reflection and Implementation Tool

How to problem solve these obstacles

My commitment to use this skill (rate 0-10):

After implementation, here is my reflection on how this worked for me:

Raindrop moments where I can use this skill in the future:

Final Reflections

I hope that you have enjoyed the process of reading and working through the exercises in this book. You've likely found some strategies that align with your unique style and speak to your needs. It is only by putting the book down and practicing the strategies that we notice benefits and changes in our own life.

Learning and establishing a new habit is a process. And mindfulness is a habit of mind; full of value, but fairly intangible. When the habit of mind has been to judge, label, and categorize, learning a new relationship with our world, our thoughts, and our emotions takes time. Beginner's mind is not difficult to describe but can be quite hard to practice, especially when our go-to response to strong, uncomfortable emotions is to allow them to dictate our behavior or squash them down in avoidance.

Habits take hold when behaviors are followed by a reinforcer. Subsequent repetitions of the behavior followed by the reinforcer cement the habit, and lead to an increase in behavioral urges to engage in the habitual behavior. I wake up sleepy and groggy from not enough sleep, I drink a double espresso and BAM!, I'm ready for the day. The feeling of alertness that ends the sleepiness is the reinforcer. The double espresso is an easy fix, and I set myself up for a morning caffeine habit.

Learning a new habit requires us to substitute a behavior to get to the desired outcome. In this example, if I wanted to break my caffeine habit, I could do things like go to bed earlier, engage in a consistent bedtime routine, and employ a variety of sleep hygiene strategies to result in waking up more refreshed and alert. To do this, I need to learn new behaviors, implement them with fidelity, resist the impulse to reinforce the old behavior (in other words, skip that coffee), and be patient as my new strategies take hold.

Much is the same with mindfulness. To collect the daily raindrops, first notice the opportunity to bring mindful awareness to task. You could substitute mindfulness practices for your mind's already learned and reinforced tendencies, perhaps moving yourself into a space of wisdom and values informed actions as opposed to mindless engagement in habits.

If you've implemented a few of the strategies from this book, bravo! As you continue to practice them, you'll likely find additional opportunities to bring mindful awareness to bear on your daily life, collecting raindrops as they appear. You may also enjoy returning to some of the other practices that you have not made habit, and exploring how they fit with your newfound mindfulness skills.

You also may have noticed something unexpected, and perhaps initially disappointing. Mindfulness practices are not a silver-bullet for life's difficulties and disappointments. I'm wrapping up work on this manuscript as we approach the one-year mark of the Covid-19 pandemic. Coincidentally as I type this, it has been exactly eleven months since I've worked in my office, face to face with my clients. It's been a difficult year for a multitude of reasons for most every person I've encountered. Mindfulness helps, but it does not change the reality: sometimes life is quite difficult.

There is a Buddhist expression, "Before enlightenment, chop wood, carry water; after enlightenment, chop wood, carry water." In other words, enlightenment does not change the realities of our day-to-day existence. We still have chores to complete, complicated interpersonal situations to manage, and uncomfortable emotional experiences like sadness, disappointment, and grief. The change is not to the life outside of us; the change is to the life within us. We change our perspective to one that decreases our attachment to expected outcomes. In other words, we practice non-judgment. The task itself (chopping wood, carrying water) is just a task requiring planning and muscle control, easily learned, and not inherently unpleasant. The judging mind (why am I stuck chopping wood and carrying water?) is the creator of the unpleasantness, and that same mind is capable of releasing this judgment.

Live your life, the full spectrum of beautiful, painful, predictable, and chaotic, bringing mindful awareness to your experiences in raindrop-sized chunks wherever you can. Add a new skill, strategy, or experience to your repertoire, perhaps on a Monday, or whenever the inspiration arises. May you soon be dancing in the rain and noticing the unbelievable opportunities for connection, curiosity, and joy that surround us at every moment. Namaste.

Acknowledgments

I am grateful and privileged to have a generous support team around me, allowing me the creative freedom to pursue writing and to strengthen and share my work. These words on paper cannot convey the magnitude of my thanks.

Many thanks go to my family, first and foremost. My husband, Jeremiah, for always supporting me personally and professionally, for being my first reader, for going along with all of my newest interests (plant stand anyone?) and, well, for everything. My children, Caden, Rowan, and Cillian, for being wonderful growing humans. It is as delightful to have "grown up" and "kid adult" conversations with you now as it was to watch you discover the world as little ones. To my parents, Sylvia and Ronald, for instilling a love of learning and the confidence to follow my dreams.

Special thanks to Melissa Devaney, Jennifer Dolan, Mimi Duff, Heidi Sauder, and Carol Tyler for serving as initial readers. Your feedback was invaluable and I truly appreciate your time and thoughtfulness.

To all my advanced readers and book ambassadors: I am grateful beyond measure. Thank you for championing *Mindful Mondays*!

A huge thank you to coach extraordinaire Lee Chaix McDonough for guidance, wisdom, support, and cheerleading. Many thanks to my peers and colleagues both in the mental health and coaching spaces for sharing knowledge.

To the people behind the book that helped it come to life: Erin Kaiser, amazing assistant and publicist; Debra Baethge, copy editor; Michele Johns at Michele Johns Photography, for a fun photoshoot and gorgeous photos; and to all the unnamed other people who have supported the journey of this book.

About the Author

Dr. Kimberly Dwyer is a clinical psychologist practicing in suburban Denver and offering telehealth throughout PsyPact states. Working from a mindfulness-based cognitive behavioral orientation (MB-CBT) and using the framework of Acceptance and Commitment Therapy (ACT), she excels at the treatment of anxiety, stress, and transforming transitional times into opportunities for growth, alignment, and self-authentication. Her background includes practice in a wealth of settings, including school, inpatient/residential, community-based, and private practice. Dr. Dwyer also supports mental health providers and similar helpers and healers in private practice to launch, grow, and re-define their businesses using values aligned intentions through a branch of her work entitled Intentional Private Practice. When she's not at work, you might find her enjoying the beautiful Colorado outdoors with her husband and three children, playing with her dogs and foster dogs, on her yoga mat, writing, or with a watercolor brush in hand.

For more information and access to additional, exclusive content for readers, visit her website at www.drkimdwyer.com/books.

Made in the USA
Monee, IL
03 September 2022

13172381R00129